BEATING THE WORKPLACE BULLY

A Tactical Guide to Taking Charge

LYNNE CURRY

Foreword by Gary Namie, Ph.D.

AMACOM
American Management Association
New York ▮ Atlanta ▮ Brussels ▮ Chicago ▮ Mexico City ▮ San Francisco
Shanghai ▮ Tokyo ▮ Toronto ▮ Washington, D.C.

Bulk discounts available. For details visit:
www.amacombooks.org/go/specialsales
Or contact special sales:
Phone: 800-250-5308
Email: specialsls@amanet.org
View all the AMACOM titles at: www.amacombooks.org
American Management Association: www.amanet.org

Library of Congress Cataloging-in-Publication Data

Curry, Lynne (Management consultant), author.
Beating the workplace bully : a tactical guide to taking charge / Lynne Curry ;
foreword by Gary Namie, Ph.D.
pages cm
Includes index.
ISBN 978-0-8144-3688-2 (pbk.) — ISBN 978-0-8144-3689-9 (ebook)
1. Bullying in the workplace. 2. Problem employees. 3. Personnel management. I. Title.
HF5549.5.E43C867 2016
658.3'82–dc23

2015030407

About AMA

American Management Association (www.amanet.org) is a world leader in talent development, advancing the skills of individuals to drive business success. Our mission is to support the goals of individuals and organizations through a complete range of products and services, including classroom and virtual seminars, webcasts, webinars, podcasts, conferences, corporate and government solutions, business books, and research. AMA's approach to improving performance combines experiential learning—learning through doing—with opportunities for ongoing professional growth at every step of one's career journey.

Printing number
10 9 8 7 6 5 4 3 2 1

To

Ben, Jenny, and Ma'Hayla, and,

like the rest of my life's work, to God.

To show the courage of your convictions requires you to have convictions.

—Doug Rice

CONTENTS

FOREWORD

The Workplace Bullying Institute's 2014 U.S. Workplace Bullying Survey documents that 65.7 million working Americans either experience or witness abusive conduct during their workday. Despite this, bullying remains a "we don't talk about that" topic, making it the "silent epidemic." Lynne Curry has plenty to say that breaks the silence. In this book, she makes it clear that the shame-targeted individual's experience is undeserved. In this practical book, she sheds light on the phenomenon and provides aggressive steps a targeted worker can take to stop the bullying.

Lynne, once a target herself, brings to the topic an overflowing bushel of tips, tools, and strategies that only a veteran workplace coach could bring. She leads you on a challenging journey made treacherous by obstacles put there by coworkers, supervisors, executives, and even society. It's an uphill battle for bullied individuals to be sure, but Lynne's realistic steps give the reader the best chance to succeed, which she defines as getting to safety with one's dignity intact—a worthy goal.

You will especially love the vivid case descriptions illustrating a different aspect of bullying that open each chapter. Lynne is a superb writer. In her abbreviated but fluid style, she manages to infuse sufficient detail to make several points at the same time. You will recognize the familiar tactics of perpetrators, targets, witnesses, and managers. Soon you'll be putting faces on those she describes because you know someone who did the exact things Lynne portrays in this book.

At the Workplace Bullying Institute, we have heard and read more stories about people targeted by bullies than any other group in the country. Lynne's anecdotes, woven together with strands from different cases, are completely authentic and believable. Some skeptics might not believe the outrageousness of some tactics she depicts, but they actually do happen as Lynne describes.

Lynne tells us that her approach is based on learning and memory theories, but in her consulting practice, as well as in this book, she eschews theory, preferring to give us practical examples. As she says, this book is a personal training manual not a recitation of theories. The welcome change is that Lynne not only teaches us "what" targets can do but also compels us to dig in, to engage, to rehearse the suggested tactics so we can get to the "how."

It's so refreshing to see an author admit that there is a huge gap between knowing and doing. I credit this to Lynne's unique perspective as a workplace coach. She obviously learned that her effectiveness depends on whether the person she advises can implement her suggestions to make sustainable changes. Brilliant delivery of advice does not guarantee efficacy, but Lynne wants readers to succeed.

For this reason, she ends each chapter with "Your Turn," a list of questions and exercises. The questions make the learning memorable by engaging simultaneously the reader's intellect, emotions, and physical actions. Please don't skip these exercises; they make this book special.

I heartily endorse the author's technique. In the early days, I learned the hard way what not to do when advising targets about workplace bullying. Back then we offered free advice to bullied workers who reached us on a toll-free line. Targets typically spent a long time describing their horrific experiences. I'd listen, then launch into a lengthy list of suggestions that I considered brilliant. At about item number twelve on a list of twenty things to do, and some forty-five minutes into the call, the caller would interrupt my monologue to ask whether to get a pencil to write down the advice. Wow—ingratitude, I thought. But I was wrong to assume that emotionally injured people could calmly follow complex instructions.

Dr. Ruth Namie, my wife, whose case launched the U.S. workplace bullying movement, taught me to stop bombarding targets with advice they were temporarily incapable of comprehending. I learned to tailor the complexity of my advice to the targets' capabilities. The "Your Turn" section of each chapter ensures that the reader is not overwhelmed.

Lynne is immersed in real-world problem solving. Her preference for directness leaps off the page. Her education and background certainly qualify her to understand and formulate theories. However, what I most appreciate is her ability to translate abstractions into actionable steps that effect change for her coaching clients. It is her most important contribution to the field. Lucky readers of this book will benefit from that talent.

Lynne brings considerable how-to experience to handling bullying and helping targets, bullies, and organizations. She writes a Q & A newspaper column in which she summarizes complex workplace dilemmas and offers sage advice to help those who write in to free themselves from the situations. The wisdom contained in this book derives partly from answering those tough bullying-related questions. Bullying problems are among the most resistant to easy solutions. Sadly, they are incredibly common. The 2014 national prevalence survey found that 27 percent of adult Americans have personally experienced abusive conduct at work.

I am delighted by Lynne's sensitivity to the plight of bullied targets, who never invited the misery dumped on them. She never condescends. Rather than victim blaming, she delivers good advice showing readers how to shore up personal vulnerabilities that bullies may use to justify an attack. Most of the book's chapters are devoted to understanding why targets become targets and showing them how to empower themselves to wrest control of their lives back from the bullies.

Though there are multiple explanations for why bullies bully, Lynne is no apologist for bullies. She deserves a great deal of credit for not falling into the trap common to myopic, less capable coaches: blaming victims and being conned by charismatic Machiavellian bullies and their executive sponsors. She clearly states that bullies have a conscience "with as many holes as a thin slice of Swiss cheese." This book is target-centric.

The concluding chapters telescope back from the interpersonal dyad of target and bully to prescribe what the employer should be doing. Here Lynne brings the same confidence that something is possible and doable that she granted to targeted individuals. According to one of our Institute's studies, 68 percent of C-suite dwellers considered workplace bullying "a serious problem." In practice, however, there is a knowing–doing gap. Despite their awareness, employers are doing relatively nothing. Lynne Curry, as executive coach, patiently explains what employers could and should do.

The author, like me, remains optimistic that the scourge of destructive bullying in the workplace can be corrected and prevented. She is positive that targets can do much to minimize damage from bullying if only they knew what to do. Fortunately for them, this book delivers many practical strategies to make their work lives safer.

Lynne Curry deserves thanks from all of us who have ever been targeted or ever attempted to make targeted individuals whole again to enjoy their lives.

Gary Namie, Ph.D.
Cofounder and Director,
Workplace Bullying Institute

ACKNOWLEDGMENTS

I could not have written this book without friends. Sally Bremner, joined by her husband, Trevor, is the beta reader/editor of my dreams; she proofread every page with unfailing enthusiasm. Deb Krebs stands out as an inspirational beta reader. Chris Lundgren added a perceptive eye to the beta reading team. Rick Birdsall added value as attorney turned human resources expert.

INTRODUCTION

INTIMIDATED NO MORE—YOU CAN DO IT

If you could get up the courage to begin, you have the courage to succeed.

—DAVID VISCOTT, MD

ANNE DIDN'T HAVE WARNING. When she landed what she thought was a dream job, she quickly bonded with a charismatic coworker, Karla. When Karla poured wine liberally at an informal dinner at her home and said, "Tell me all about you," Anne did.

The next day, the receptionist giggled as Anne walked in. When Anne asked, "What's so funny?" the receptionist looked at her, wide-eyed, and squeaked, "Nothing."

Later, as Anne entered the break room for a cup of coffee, two of her new coworkers abruptly stopped talking.

At the afternoon staff meeting, she noticed two male coworkers smirking at her.

Anne went home with a headache, and decided to cheer herself up by logging on to Facebook. To her horror, she discovered that her coworkers were posting wildly exaggerated stories about her past relationships—all based on her private conversation with Karla. With her heart-shaped face ashen and her fists clenched so tight that the blood had wrung out of them, she called Karla. No answer.

The next day, Anne confronted Karla, who gave her a cold, coyote smile, and replied, "I have no idea what you're talking about."

"But the things they're posting could only have come from you," Anne insisted, nausea percolating in her stomach.

"Pull yourself together," Karla snapped. "You clearly have issues."

Anne endured three more weeks of sideways glances, during which Karla tormented her with her own stories about unsuccessful love and work relationships. When Anne finally turned to Craigslist to find a new job, she discovered that her personal stories had circulated throughout the industry.

That's when I met Anne. She described Karla, a two-faced Dr. Jekyll/Ms. Hyde, and shared how Karla had manipulated her into divulging personal details that, repeated out of context, made Anne look like a fool.

"Is there anything I can do?" she asked. "My female coworkers think I'm a bad joke. They look at me as if I'm something they scraped off the bottom of their shoes. The guys in my office, including my boss, are scared I'm man hungry, and make a point of telling me they love their wives."

"What do they think about Karla?" I asked.

"They don't like her, but no one crosses her. She has a power that I can't explain. It's like everyone goes along with her so she doesn't attack them."

"How have you fought back?" I asked.

"I haven't."

"Which means that as far as Karla's concerned it's open season on you. What's your boss doing about this?"

"Nothing. It's as if she has something on him."

"Bullies win," I explained, "because they set a rigged game in motion, and the rest of us find ourselves playing it—and badly. If you want to escape the bully's control, you need to take the bully on and change the game's rules."

WHAT THIS BOOK PROMISES YOU

Workplace bullies. Have you recently tangled with one? Did you hold your own or did the bully ride roughshod over you? Do you expect a rematch?

If you've picked up this book, you want a better result the next time you encounter your bully. You want to walk away feeling whole, not trampled.

That's what *Beating the Workplace Bully* offers you. In each chapter, you'll find concrete strategies, skills, and tools for successfully outmaneuvering bullies in your workplace.

You'll learn:

- How to quell your instinctive fear and not feel intimidated
- Powerful strategies to use with those who intimidate you
- Methods for turning the tables on bullies
- Strategies for building self-confidence
- Bully traps to avoid
- How to engage your fighting spirit
- Strategic moves for handling feared or unexpected attacks
- How to keep bullies from gaining an outpost in your mind
- Ways to calm yourself in any confrontation
- How to strengthen your "fighting-back" muscles
- The truth and falseness in bully myths and assumptions
- How to keep your dignity intact

. . . along with the steps employers, supervisors, and managers can take to successfully derail and prevent bullies from trampling on their employees.

In addition to learning how to handle yourself around any bully, you'll have the opportunity to assess your current personal conflict style and decide on the changes you want to make. At the end of each chapter, you'll have the opportunity to put your bully situation into perspective, or try out your new skills with practical exercises. You can count on *Beating the Workplace Bully* to provide you with the tactics you need to change how you handle bullies.

WHAT I PROMISE YOU

From me, as your personal coach, you can expect someone who partners with you. In the past, you may have enjoyed a book that promised similar benefits and thought "I wish I could really do what the author is telling me to do." Then, you set the book aside, never putting what you read into practice. I want more for you.

Beating the Workplace Bully offers you more than most books; it's your personal training manual. In it I go beyond explaining "what" to do; I teach you "how" to do it.

Research shows that while you remember only 10 percent of what you read, you retain 70 percent of what you answer if immediately questioned about what you've learned. Even better, if you try out or put into practice the skills or knowledge you've just learned, you retain 90 percent of that information eight months after learning it.[1]

Research also reveals that nothing encodes in memory unless you encode it in at least two of the three ways you mentally process information: visually (you see it), auditorily (you discuss it or say it out loud), and kinesthetically (you try it out physically or emotionally process it). That's why you often have to repeat major life lessons over and over—because they're insights and not retained unless verbalized, worked with, or otherwise implemented.[2]

Beating the Workplace Bully addresses this issue by actively involving you at the end of each chapter with questions and activities that help you retain the new approach to handling bullies covered in that chapter. In "Your Turn: Where Are You Now?" you'll learn exactly how to defeat a bully, and get the chance to put your new skills into practice.

Why choose me as your personal coach? Since 1978 I've run an employee training, management, and human resources consulting firm that serves 3,500 clients in fourteen states and three countries. I have a Ph.D. in social psychology and an MA in teaching and am a certified Senior Professional in Human Resources.

Every month I teach individuals—as a personal coach or in group sessions—how to handle workplace bullies. Many of my clients call these seminars life-changing.

Every strategy that you read in *Beating the Workplace Bully* has been field-tested.

Based on my background as a manager and employee trainer, I've created this one-on-one training session that you can complete in the privacy of your own home or office.

You'll read dramatic real-life stories about individuals targeted by bullies, as well as about the bullies themselves. You'll learn from real-world situations facing individuals, like yourself, who fell into traps bullies set for them. You'll gain insight when you read how they sprung and then climbed out of those traps.

Bullies and targets exist at all levels and in many organizations. These real-life examples are culled from my thirty-seven years of helping others learn how to successfully outsmart the bullies. That said, no anecdote represents any one individual. In all instances, each is a composite of two or three of the many targets and bullies I've coached merged into one story. I have changed the names and specific facts out of respect for those I've coached. You will likely find a bully who's a dead ringer for one you've tangled with—and then find special pleasure in learning how to turn the tables on this bully. One last note: Although many of the bullies and bullied in these anecdotes are women, it is important to remember that bullies and targets come in male and female form as well as all ages, shapes, and disguises.

I've told you my professional credentials, but what about my personal credentials? I've been bullied myself, but I am no longer a victim. I married—and divorced—a bully. I even employed bullies. When I decided I'd had enough, I looked in vain for a book that would help, and then made the decision to study bullies in my life and in the lives of clients I helped. In that way, I learned the many ways in which I'd been an easy mark.

Once I understood that, I was never again on the losing end of bullying. The book in your hands is the book I would have wanted to read. What this means for you is that I'm uniquely positioned and excited to be your coach.

I'm delighted that you're taking this journey, one that could dramatically change your life for the better. The rewards ahead of you are priceless.

Your Turn: Where Are You Now?

1. Are you currently entangled with a bully?
2. Describe the bully. (For example, how does she or he act? What has she or he done to you? How have you reacted? How has she or he made you feel?)
3. What happened? (For example, how did you react? Did you withdraw or fight back and, if so, how? How did your coworkers or supervisors act? What's the current situation?)
4. What do you hope to learn or gain as a result of reading *Beating the Workplace Bully*?

NOTES

1. Merrill Harmin and Melanie Toth, *Inspiring Active Learning: A Complete Handbook for Today's Teachers* (Alexandria, VA: Association for Supervision and Curriculum Development, 2006), 230; Sharon Hull, *Making Comprehension Connections: Look, Listen, and Link!* (Huntington Beach, CA: Shell Education, 2008),

The Peak Performance Center, http://thepeakperformancecenter.com/educational-learning/learning/principles-of-learning/learning-pyramid/.

2. Dharma Singh Khalsa and Cameron Stauth, *Brain Longevity: The Breakthrough Medical Program that Improves Your Mind and Memory* (New York: Warner Books, 1999).

1

ARE YOU A BULLY MAGNET?

Courage is knowing what not to fear.

—PLATO

HEAD NURSE MOLLY was ten months from retirement when Pauline started work at the clinic. Like the rest of the clinic's employees, Molly welcomed Pauline aboard, greeting her with flowers on her first day. Pauline took the flowers with barely a glance and handed them to the receptionist, saying "Put these in water."

Molly, a kind, round-faced woman with warm hazel eyes and wavy auburn hair flecked with gray, had urged the clinic's physician owners to hire someone like Pauline, saying the clinic had grown to a size that required a clinic administrator in addition to her own head nurse position. When the managing physician asked Molly, "Do you want to supervise her?" Molly responded, "I see us as teammates, each with our strengths balancing and supporting the other."

For the next two weeks, Molly coached Pauline on the clinic's intake, staff orientation, patient recordkeeping, and administrative filing systems—all procedures she'd spent more than ten years developing.

Since Molly took pride in her work, it shocked her when Pauline described the systems as "antiquated." Molly viewed the systems as simple, streamlined, and even elegant, but she swallowed her pride and said, "I'll support you in making them better."

"Won't be necessary," Pauline sneered.

"You don't want my help?" Molly asked, thinking she'd misunderstood Pauline's tone.

"I don't *need* your help," Pauline replied in a voice that could curdle milk.

That night, Molly attended Pauline's first briefing with the clinic's physicians, and listened as Pauline told them that bringing clinic systems and procedures up to an acceptable level would take four to six months of hard work as things were in a "pitiful" state. Pauline looked the part of someone who could take the clinic forward. She dressed in immaculate and stylish, if severe, suits.

Molly's jaw dropped and ice formed in her gut as Pauline continued to trash her work. Molly didn't know what to say in defense of the clinic's existing systems, and couldn't bear to make eye contact with the physicians she'd served for twenty years.

The next morning, the stream of insulting emails started. Although Molly tried to focus on her head nurse duties, she felt obligated to respond to the three or four daily emails outlining in detail errors Pauline alleged Molly had made when she designed the clinic's systems.

Molly worked ten-hour days until deep shadows formed under her eyes. She finally asked for a meeting with Pauline. Pauline's new assistant, Max, turned her down, telling Molly that Pauline's schedule was "tight."

Molly went home drained, and told her husband she had no idea why Pauline was attacking everything she'd developed.

"Why are you letting this woman do this to you?" asked Molly's husband.

"She has the credentials the physicians wanted."

"You've worked for them for twenty years."

"She says she knows what she's doing."

"So do you."

Molly wasn't so sure anymore.

The next day, Molly saw three emails from Pauline and realized she didn't want to open any of them.

How had things turned from great to trash?

WHAT MADE YOU A VICTIM? WHAT KEEPS YOU A VICTIM?

If a bully has you in his or her crosshairs, you may look at yourself and wonder if you're to blame, and for what. You want to know what made you a target.

Let's turn that around and look at what bullying is.

Workplace Bullying Defined

Workplace bullying is *psychological violence* and *aggressive manipulation* in the form of repeated humiliation or intimidation, and may include situational, verbal, or physical abuse.

- **Verbal bullying** includes slandering, ridiculing, insulting or persistent hurtful name-calling, and making the target the butt of jokes or abusive, offensive remarks.
- **Physical bullying** includes pushing, shoving, kicking, poking, or tripping the target. It also includes making obscene gestures as well as assault or the threat of physical assault.
- **Situational bullying** involves sabotage and cruel acts of deliberate humiliation and interference.

Workplace bullying and harassment can inflict serious harm upon targeted employees, including feelings of shame, humiliation, anxiety, and depression, along with physical symptoms of distress.

No one deserves to be bullied.

Even if you've done many things wrong, even if your self-esteem isn't the greatest, even if you've made a hundred mistakes, don't take what the bully dishes out as your due.

Bullying is an epidemic. According to a 2014 VitalSmarts survey, 96 percent of the study's 2,283 respondents experienced workplace bullying.[1] The 2014 U.S. Workplace Bullying Survey published by the Workplace Bullying Institute documents that 37 million U.S. workers face "abusive conduct" during their workday. Another 28.7 million witness this abuse.[2] To put this into perspective, these 65.6 million people equal the combined population of fifteen U.S. states from the central northern tier to the Gulf of Mexico.

At a minimum, three to four people out of every ten have been bullied. You may well ask, "Can't I please be one of the other six or seven of those ten?"

Absolutely, that's why you're reading this book.

Your first step is to recognize which of the following factors led you into a bully's crosshairs.

You:

- Have bad luck
- Ignore warning signs
- Have something the bully wants
- Signal you're an easy target
- Put up with lousy treatment
- Give away your power

Bad Luck: A Target on Your Back

A MILITARY WIFE, Gwen interviewed for five weeks before finding an employer willing to hire her despite her husband's likely transfer to a new base in eighteen months.

On Gwen's first day on the job, Lisa, the office manager, sat her down and told her she'd do fine if she understood the lay of the land. Eager to make a good impression, Gwen listened to Lisa, who explained that Gwen needed to demonstrate her willingness to be a team player.

Gwen was soon spending hours completing tasks Lisa delegated to her, which prevented her from speedily completing assignments given her by her immediate supervisor. When Gwen told Lisa she couldn't manage the extra tasks, Lisa snapped, "You're not willing to help me out when I'm swamped?"

Gwen hadn't been bullied before, and she took days to decide what to do. She spoke to her supervisor, who said, "Lisa's our best, most talented performer. I can't believe you're bad-mouthing her when she's been trying to help you." As Gwen listened in shock, her fists tightly closed and shoved into her pockets, she learned that Lisa had claimed that Gwen came to her so often for help that Lisa had to log two hours overtime nightly to complete her own assignments.

Landing the wrong job had placed Gwen in a bully's crosshairs. Has bad luck made you a bully's target?

Ignore Warning Signs at Your Peril

AFTER A DIVORCE, Mack moved to Colorado and took the first job offered him. When he saw a long list of names as he logged on to Outlook, he asked a coworker about them. "I'm new here too," she said, "I don't recognize any of them."

On his first day, Mack's boss took him out to a five-star restaurant for lunch. "Slow service!" his boss snarled at the waitress, "If you want a tip, speed it up." Minutes later, his boss snapped his fingers as the waitress passed by, "Coffee refill!"

At the weekly staff meeting, Mack was surprised that few employees talked, other than to compliment their boss when he spoke about his personal efforts. Their silence made Mack hesitant to talk. After the meeting, he asked a coworker, "How come no one talks?" "You'll learn," she responded. "We go along to get along. No one sticks their neck out."

As Mack delved into the projects assigned him, several of his clients asked him what had happened to different people who'd worked with them before Mack joined the company. Mack soon learned not to ask his boss about his predecessors; they'd all left on bad terms.

Although Mack liked his salary, he decided that working for this boss could prove a career-fatal mistake. He saw the warning signs and left before his boss turned on him.

What about you? Have you seen similar warning signs? Have you bailed out in time or stayed too long?

Potential Warning Signs

You work with an individual who:

- ☐ Cuts you down, then claims she was "just kidding"
- ☐ Makes you feel like you "walk on eggshells" because you never know what might trigger a tirade
- ☐ Holds past employees, employers, or coworkers responsible for his unhappiness
- ☐ Hates to have her authority questioned
- ☐ Treats others poorly when he can get away with it
- ☐ Delights in making your life difficult
- ☐ Intimidates you or others
- ☐ Puts you in the wrong so she can make herself appear right

Beware: What the Bully Wants, the Bully Gets

LAURA BUILT HER business from scratch while living on rice, beans, and peanut butter. Over years of sixty-hour workweeks, she'd created essential materials for anyone who wanted to launch a successful business in her field.

Through her hard work and passion about the services she provided her clients, Laura made a name for herself. Clients sought her out, and her business produced a growing profit. She hired an administrative assistant and focused on providing her clients with top-quality work.

When Laura decided to grow her business, she hired Martin and committed herself to helping him develop.

Despite Laura's generosity, Martin envied how clients viewed his boss. He wanted her reputation for himself. He took Laura's name and copyright off original materials she'd developed, and replaced them with his own. He bad-mouthed her to clients.

When Laura called Martin on his actions, he smiled an alligator smile, and said, "So sad, too bad, see you around" and walked out the door before she could fire him. After Martin left, Laura not only spent weeks cleaning up the messes Martin made, she also learned that Martin had solicited her best clients for his planned new business.

Although some clients hadn't liked Martin, several asked, "Were you asleep at the wheel?" Laura soon realized that allowing Martin too much latitude before she got to know him tarnished her reputation along with Martin's.

In the weeks that followed, several clients called Laura sharing the stories Martin had told them about her, alleging she'd come on to him sexually, and fired him when he'd turned her down. Though few clients believed these stories, just hearing them made Laura sick to her stomach.

Then the tweets and blog postings from myriad email accounts started coming. Posters Laura didn't know and couldn't trace accused her of lying about her degree, sleeping with clients, and stealing others' work and passing it off as her own. Laura, who had loved going to work and interacting with clients in person and on social media, soon dreaded answering the phone or logging on to Twitter.

One by one, Laura's clients left her, in part because she never regained her fighting spirit, allowing Martin to "steal" the reputation he envied.

Has a bully come after you because you had something he or she wanted?

On the Radar: An Easy Target

SONJA WAS INEXPERIENCED and new to the workplace, so she kept to herself. Her tremulous voice and slender build gave her an air of permanent fragility. She worked alongside Alice, who excelled at sniping. "Look who forgot to button her blouse," Alice quipped when Sonja walked into the staff meeting. When Sonja reddened, Alice snickered, "Look who's gullible!"

As Sonja cast her eyes down, Alice continued to bait her. "Looking at your photo badge," she proclaimed, grabbing the photo ID on the lanyard around Sonja's neck. "I would too. That's an awful picture. Go back to HR and make them take it again!"

Sonja, reeling from the public attack and unable to think of how to handle it, sat in frozen silence during the short staff meeting, even though the topic was one in which she had a keen interest. Alice, however, spoke out, scoring points with the corporate executive who chaired the meeting.

When Sonja returned to her desk, she put her head down. She'd let Alice attack her without defending herself.

Like Sonja, do you signal you're an easy target? Bullies read people for a living, choosing vulnerable individuals who wear their sensitivity on their sleeves as targets.

Are You an Easy Target?

Questions to ask yourself include:

- ☐ Are you meek?

- ◻ Would you rather submit to bad treatment than engage in conflict?
- ◻ Have you made the mistake of letting the wrong person know you were exploited in a prior job?
- ◻ Does past personal trauma haunt you, causing you to freeze when confronted?
- ◻ Are you socially isolated, without work allies to back you up and ward off a bully's attacks?
- ◻ Do others consider you unlikely to confront them if they tread on you?
- ◻ Do you signal vulnerability in other ways?

If you answered "yes" to any of these questions, bullies may find you on their radar.

If You Let Them, They Will Do It: Lousy Treatment

THE FIRST TIME Andy barked at Annette, she raised an eyebrow and asked, "Bad day? Would you prefer I come back later?" "Let's do it," he snarled. "You people push for this and push for that. You think you're the only people who count. What's this f---ing email you sent all about?" Annette got up and left his office.

Andy sent her a stormy email, which she forwarded to their supervisor and Human Resources. The next day, a chastened Andy responded with the information Annette had requested.

By contrast, Annette's predecessor, Suzanne, stayed put despite Andy's tirades, even when he called her a "f---ing bitch." Convinced she needed Andy's information to complete her report, Suzanne endured meetings in which a red-faced Andy screamed in her face. When Suzanne finally quit, others asked why she had put up with it for so long. Suzanne answered, "I kept thinking it would get better."

Do bullies target you because you let them?

Don't pass the test you should fail. Bullies eat nice people alive. They test to see if you'll allow bad treatment and, if you do, they escalate their abuse.

Just Say "No": Give Away Your Power

AFTER LEAVING HER last job to get away from a bully, Tova hoped for a fresh start in her new position as an inside sales professional. Her new boss, Buck, told her she'd support the rest of the sales team, and also have her own clients.

"Will they mind that I've never done sales?" Tova asked.

"We're hiring you for your administrative support skills, essential for success in inside sales. Besides, you'll have Arielle, the other woman on the team, to help you get the hang of things."

The problems began her first day. As Tova headed to her desk, Arielle asked, "You like coffee?" "I love it," answered Tova. "Great," said Arielle. "When you grab yours from the cart in the lobby, I want a café latte grande with caramel."

Not sure what the customs were on her new team, Tova said "Sure," and headed to the cart. When she handed Arielle her $5 drink, Arielle, who was on the phone, waved her away, mouthing, "Busy."

Tova expected Arielle to reciprocate with coffee the next morning. Arielle didn't. Instead, when Arielle saw Tova heading for the coffee cart, Arielle called out, "My usual." Tova didn't want to make waves, and knew she needed Arielle's guidance to become a success, so she bought Arielle a second latte. And a third.

Tova never received guidance from Arielle. Once, when Tova handed Arielle a draft proposal and asked, "I'd like your thoughts on this," Arielle responded, "Do you know your name is a four-letter word?"

As Tova's jaw dropped, Arielle said, "You asked my thoughts. That's what I thought."

Shocked, Tova said, "That hurts!"

"Oh, poor baby," Arielle goaded, smiling at another employee. "Toughen up."

While others on the sales team weren't the bully Arielle was, they soon learned that if they asked, "Hey, Tova, could you . . . ," she would say, "Sure." That didn't mean they helped Tova when Arielle belittled her. Instead, the others, like Arielle, gave Tova the grunt work projects they didn't want. Although Tova knew the requests were unreasonable, she did what they asked.

Like Tova, do you have no power, or do you have "no" power? If you're tired of being a doormat, you owe it to yourself to say "no more" or "stop" when a bully takes advantage of you or puts you down. If you allow disrespectful treatment, you hand over your power.

Your Turn: Where Are You Now?

1. What in the past put you in a bully's crosshairs? Which of the six factors fits you?
2. Into what category does head nurse Molly fit? What mistakes did she make?
3. If you've had bad luck, how do you plan to make it change? If you are unable to change your situation, how can you change your responses to the bullying in a way that doesn't feed the bully's desire to hurt or demean you?
4. Have you ignored warning signs? If so, which? What have you learned for next time?
5. Has a bully come after you because you had something the bully wanted? If so, have you let the bully take it away? Is there a way you can regain what was yours?
6. Are there ways in which you signal that you are an easy target?

7. You're a walking history of everything that's happened to you until you decide to rewrite your history. Are there past incidents that have made you vulnerable to bullying? Write two of them on a piece of paper, then describe what you want your pattern to be in the future.
8. Have you given away your power as Molly and Tova did? Name one way in which you can immediately start to take your power back. Put your decision into action within the week.

Some of these questions may have stirred up past emotions. Which ones? Shame? Sadness? Anger? Despair? Tell yourself you can let go of those feelings, that you don't need to keep holding them inside. When you are hurt, you may find yourself holding onto the hurt. You may feel that if you can figure it out, it won't be as painful. Unfortunately, you often hurt yourself all over again when you think about an experience that drags you down. If that's the case, you may want to find a private place and let yourself express that feeling by crying, punching soft pillows, or shaking your fists. You may decide to journal. If that doesn't work, you may want to locate a coach or counselor in your area.

NOTES

1. Naomi Shavin, "What Workplace Bullying Looks Like in 2014—and How to Intervene," workplace bullying study by David Maxfield and Joseph Grenny, *Forbes*, June 25, 2014.
2. Gary Namie, 2014 WBI U.S. Workplace Bullying Survey, February 2014, http://www.workplacebullying.org/wbiresearch/wbi-2014-us-survey.

YOU CAN RUN, BUT YOU CAN'T HIDE

BULLIES DON'T GO AWAY ON THEIR OWN

Only those who will risk going too far can possibly find out how far one can go.

—T. S. ELIOT

"**BEING TREATED AS IF** I was a piece of crap at work took away my sense of who I was and replaced it with shame," said head nurse Molly. "I'd never met someone as cold, self-righteous, or cruel as Pauline. After weeks of being bullied, I didn't know what to do but quit."

When a bully first confronts you, you may wonder, "Why me?" The answer—while bullying says more about the bully than it does about you, you're the one who has to learn to stand up for yourself.

You may have tried to ignore a workplace bully, hoping things would get better on their own. You may believe that if you act professionally and politely, bullies will leave you alone or act nicely in return.

This ignores the truth about bullying.

You can't expect bullies to go away on their own.

Bullies perceive niceness and avoidance as weakness and an invitation to take advantage. Those who don't stand up to the bully's initial attack signal they're easy prey and inadvertently encourage continued bullying.

When someone snipes at you and you ignore it, most people take the hint, realize they are being jerks, and stop. Those folks aren't bullies.

On the other hand, if a bully insults you and you don't counter it, the bully pokes a second time, testing your boundaries. If you don't counter the second jab, you prove you're an easy target. The situation then spirals out of control, and the bullying escalates, particularly if the workplace audience rewards the bully with laughter.

You may consider bullies wrongdoers who need to fix the problems they create. In practice, the opposite is true. Even if what's happening isn't your fault, you are the one who must fix it, because you can't expect the bully to change.

You may expect to receive help from coworkers or your supervisor when under fire. However, many bullies reveal their true selves only to their target while maintaining a charming front to the rest of the world. Also, because the rest of us give the benefit of the doubt to everyone until we personally experience otherwise, bystanders rarely help those slammed by bullies. When bystanders finally realize what's going on, they may run for cover or consider the fight yours rather than theirs.

Under current law, bullying isn't illegal, unless it evolves into physical violence or is directed against employees who have "protected" status under municipal, state, or federal laws, such as Title VII of the Civil Rights Act of 1964, the Age Discrimination in Employment Act, or the Americans with Disabilities Act. Unfortunately for you and millions of other workplace bullying victims, most employers lack anti-bullying policies of their own and treat workplace bullying as if it was a dirty little secret. As a result, victims must figure out how to handle the situation on their own. If you are one of these "unprotected" victims, you may be tolerating bullying, hoping it goes away.

Are You a Victim of Bullying?

Bullies often do things that make your work life a nightmare.

- ☐ Do you walk on eggshells around an individual with a hair-trigger temper?
- ☐ Does someone you work with regularly call you vile names or insult you?
- ☐ Does a coworker, boss, or other employee intimidate you with aggressive body language or physical violence?
- ☐ Does a boss, coworker, or other employee humiliate you in front of others and/or repeatedly berate you in private?
- ☐ Does a coworker subject you to a stream of insulting emails?
- ☐ Do you work with a person who frequently criticizes you in public because he or she knows you won't fight back?

If so, you may have shut your eyes to the fact you're being bullied.

Further, others in your workplace may encourage you to compromise with the bully. They may question whether you're making things up or creating the problem. They may abandon or betray you. You may feel you stand alone—and that may be true.

Many victims internalize bullying, feeling they somehow deserve the treatment they receive. You may wonder what's wrong with you or why you can't handle the situation.

If you're experiencing bullying, you're not to blame.

If you take what a bully says or does personally, or allow disrespectful treatment, you collude with the bully and abdicate your responsibility to yourself. Don't let bullies stomp on your spirit or invite themselves into your head.

If, however, you successfully handle yourself and the situation, others will witness a failed bullying attempt, which will allow them to see what's going on.

Your Turn: Where Are You Now?

1. Describe the bullying you've experienced—in particular, what made you initially realize you were being bullied, and how you responded.
2. Which category or categories outlined in Chapter 1 does your experience fall into?
3. How recently have you been bullied?
4. How often have you been bullied?
5. What have you tried?
6. What haven't you tried?
7. What thoughts led to your action or inaction?
8. Whom do you think bullies go after?
9. Do you think bullies feel remorse?
10. Who has witnessed the way the bully treats you? Who else has the bully targeted?
11. Are there ways in which these individuals could help you? Is there anyone else who could help or are you on your own?
12. Might you be able to describe the bullying to your supervisor or manager in terms of your company's reputation and bottom line rather than your personal hurt? If so, how?
13. If you've been hiding, how might you benefit from coming out into the open? Name one step you can take, and take it this week.

DOORMATS CAN CHANGE: HERE'S WHAT IT TAKES

Courage is being scared to death
but saddling up anyway.

—JOHN WAYNE

ADAM'S PROMOTION TOOK GEOFF by surprise. Geoff, a tall, good-looking "golden boy" with a penchant for expensive, tailored suits, had thought the promotion was his as he'd worked for the company longer, had an advanced degree, and considered himself more talented than his coworkers.

Adam, a slender, Asian-American man with a gentle face, reached out to Geoff and the other employees after his promotion, saying, "I want us to be a team." Bitter, Geoff rebuffed Adam, making it clear he planned to stay in the job only because he needed the income, adding, "Hope you don't f--- things up too bad."

Adam didn't respond and didn't mention this conversation to his boss because he wanted his boss to think he could handle the challenges of a newly promoted supervisor.

Adam's silence emboldened Geoff. Each week Geoff emailed Adam a "helpful" critique of Adam's actions as manager, copying Adam's boss. Adam wasn't sure how to handle these emails, as Geoff cloaked his comments in statements of apparent concern for the department's future.

Over the next months, Geoff openly questioned Adam's decisions in conversations with other team members. At team meetings, he asserted himself so forcefully that he usurped the leadership role. Adam didn't put a stop to any of this because he hated conflict and hoped things would settle down.

PROBLEMS DON'T *JUST* GO AWAY

If you're like Adam, you wait for problems to fade away by themselves. You hope staying out of the bully's way solves the problem. Perhaps you're a person who'd rather work things out than argue. The idea of fighting back when attacked may even make you feel sick. It may be that in your family, no one called bullying what it is.

Can you learn to stand up for yourself? You bet. Your past doesn't predict your future, unless *you* bring the past with you. Which you will, *unless you consciously decide to change.*

Let me show you how this can happen to you unless you make a midcourse correction.

Try this experiment. Intertwine your arms as if you're pretzeling them and notice which hand comes out on top. Then, re-cross your arms so your other hand comes out on top. You may find this second position awkward to do and uncomfortable to maintain. That's because when you crossed your arms the first time and one hand came out on top, you initiated a pattern. If the same hand came out on top the next two times you crossed your arms, you locked into a consistent pattern for how you crossed your arms.

Every habit you have started with doing something and then repeating it several times. Try this experiment to see how quickly you develop habits. Spell these words out loud:

JOKE

SMOKE

FOLK

Now spell the word for the white of an egg. If you caught yourself spelling y-o-l-k instead of egg white, shell, or albumin, you spelled the word for the yellow of an egg because you had quickly formed a habit.

Similarly, if the first time an angry individual walked over you or verbally roughed you up you backed down because you didn't know how else to handle the situation, you initiated a pattern. If you backed down more than once, you developed a habit for avoiding conflict. You can change any habit you've fallen into by making and repeating new patterns, which you'll learn in Chapters 5 through 11.

THE FIRST STEP ON THE ROAD TO CHANGE

Train yourself to see new possibilities. We tend to believe that when we look at something, we see what's there. Yet do we? What do you see here?

Do you see the word *trees* or the top half of the word *trees*?
Or do you see the top half of what's really there?

Take another look:

T B 5 5 S

What do you see now?
We see what we expect to see.

Next, read this phrase aloud with its words jammed together:
Opportunity isnowhere.
How did you read it?
Opportunity is *no where* or opportunity is *now here*?

Changing your mental patterns requires seeing what's in front of your eyes and even yourself from a new and more positive perspective.

GET READY TO CHANGE: EXPAND YOUR COMFORT ZONE

Are you ready to believe you can see things in a new way? Or are you locked into your current view of yourself and your bully, even though you'd like the situation to be different and better? While you're a walking history of everything that's happened to you, as long as you live, you're not frozen in your history. You can change your habitual responses in the same way you can learn to see opportunity is *now here* rather than *nowhere.* You no longer need to allow yourself to be bullied.

The solution to handling bullying begins within you.

Here's an example of one strategy that works. Imagine that you are handling multiple tight-deadline projects given to you by two of your three supervisors. While you are completing these rush assignments, your third supervisor, a bully, gives you a new assignment, angrily barking, "Complete this immediately!"

In the past, you may have quaked inside; your face may have reddened. You may even have felt that the bully, and perhaps others listening, saw you as someone who worked too slowly. This may have hurt your feelings or embarrassed you.

Now imagine handling this differently. You take a deep breath and realize, "This bully is barking. If he were a dog, would I freeze inside or think, 'there's a barking dog'?"

If you view the bully's barking that way, you might straighten your shoulders, stand tall, and say "I'll get it done."

If the bully demands, "I need it done now!" and you hear it as simply louder barking, you can answer, "I'll get to your project as quickly as I can."

By calmly handling your bully supervisor, you may gain his respect. Bullies have more respect for those who stand up to them.

Do you have to stand up to every bully? No. You can choose which bullies to handle in new ways, what changes you'll make, and the degree to which you'll stand up to the bullies in your life. You never have to (nor should you) do something you feel is unwise or more challenging than you can handle.

Three Immediate Results of Taking the First Step

What can you expect when you stand up to a bully for the first time?

First, even if handling situations or bullies in new ways feels difficult, you can feel good about standing up for yourself.

Second, the first time you stand up to a bully generally proves to be the hardest. After that, confronting bad treatment gets easier.

Third, new habits replace old habits more quickly than you might guess, even when the old habits represent years of behavior. Have you ever noticed that most past events, no matter how vivid, fade from memory? New experiences replace them. Similarly, a new habit, even one repeated only eight times, grows stronger than an older habit not recently revisited.

THE NEXT STEP: DO IT AGAIN

When you start a new habit or behavior, you automatically build a new neurological pathway in your brain to support the habit. Each time you repeat the habit, your thoughts move across this new neural pathway.

As the new mental pathway becomes more frequently traveled, it becomes the route more likely to be instinctively traveled. Experts maintain that those who repeat a new habit for eight to twenty-one days, even with occasional relapses, form a new habit that eventually "takes over" the earlier pattern. This means the more often you handle bullies in new ways, the more those patterns become yours.

So, decide now. Do you want to create new habits and behaviors? It's up to you. You can change.

The past or the future? The choice is yours.

Your Turn: Where Are You Now?

1. Sometime in the next three days, do one thing you consider out of the ordinary. For example, approach and speak to someone you don't know. Or, if you don't normally do it, compliment someone. If neither of these suggestions places you outside your comfort zone, be creative and push yourself.
2. Do you accept being bullied even though you'd like your work life or you to be different? If so, the first step is to expand your thinking. Ask yourself: What would you like to be different in your work life? How do you want to be treated?
3. We're all complex people. We might be afraid in one area but brave in another. In what areas of your life do you now handle situations assertively and pursue what you want? If you currently face a workplace bully, what tools or beliefs from those other areas could you employ against the bully? What would it feel like to approach this situation with more confidence?
4. Choosing gives you power. This week, think of one way you can stand up for yourself and test it out. As an example, if you've shut down in the past when a bully made snarky comments, decide how you'll handle it differently the next time. What if you responded "Pardon me?" in a tone that said you couldn't believe anyone would be so rude? You may find it helpful to rehearse potential responses so that they'll come quickly to mind when you need them.
5. Have you put off confronting a bully, hoping things would get better? Did they get worse instead? How will you ben-

efit from handling the bully today, or this week, rather than next?

6. Has a bully made you feel to blame for how he or she has treated you? Would your best friend see it that way? How do you plan to get the bully's indictment of you out of your head? (In Chapter 8, I offer specific strategies for removing bullies from your mind.)
7. What's an action step you feel comfortable taking to improve your future success in handling bullies? (It might be continuing reading this book, or planning and practicing how you'll handle the next bully interaction, or talking to your supervisor about the situation. Whatever you choose, decide on an action step and take it—this week. The solution lies within you.)

WOUNDED RHINOS, SHAPE-SHIFTERS, CHARACTER ASSASSINS, AND OTHER BULLIES

You will never do anything in this world without courage. It is the greatest quality of the mind next to honor.

—ARISTOTLE

ON WHAT TURNED OUT to be Sam's last day at his job, his boss, Bernard, a stout man with tree-stump legs, a broad, glistening forehead, and a jutting jaw, sent all employees an email reading "Assemble immediately in the company lunchroom for a motivational speech." When the employees gathered, Bernard stomped in as though he was putting out small brush fires and instructed the Human Resources manager to hand an envelope to each employee. He then ordered the employees to open their envelopes.

As Sam read what was in his envelope, a printed statement listing his salary and benefits, he heard another employee mutter, "What the hell?"

"None of you deserve your paychecks," shouted Bernard, spittle spraying from his mouth. "You're unmotivated, incompetent, and deserve to be fired," As Sam stood in shock, the person next to him started to tremble; another began to cry. Bernard marched in front of the rows of employees as he spoke, jowls quivering, his face bright red.

"There is blood in the water. You'll get results or you'll be gone. Go back to your desks and prove yourselves."

Sam returned to his desk, wrote a one-sentence resignation letter, packed up his personal belongings, and left.

What leads some people to bully?

THE BULLY MINDSET

Growing up, bullies learn how to push others' emotional buttons to get what they want. Because button-pushing works, bullies discover they can get what they want through fear, guilt, or intimidation.

Bullies view the rest of the world as revolving around them and others as subservient to their self-interest. A bully thinks, "I want this and I'm going to have it," or "If I take this and you let me, it's mine." While others might do what a bully does and feel bad later or push to a certain degree but then back off, bullies lack internal brakes and enjoy exercising power over others. Bullies see themselves as the center of their universe, rationalize their behavior, and feel confident and justified in what they do.

Many wonder if bullies are born that way or made. The answer appears to be "made," though several personality disorders—narcissism and antisocial and obsessive-compulsive personality disorders—overlap with classic bully types.

When confronted, most bullies state, "This is just the way I am," and while many bullies and those who work with them believe this, bullies also think, "Why should I change? What I'm doing works for me." Bullies rarely examine their own behavior. Ask a bully why he exploded in rage and he'll say you made him do it because you screwed up, challenged him, or stood in the way of him implementing his vision. Bullies may even brag about expressing anger instead of bottling up emotions. This lack of guilt, empathy, or compassion means that bullies rarely change voluntarily.

Bullies feel no remorse, believing that those who don't have their savvy, ambition, strength, or aggression deserve to be walked over. Pleading with or trying to appease bullies backfires as bullies have little respect for those they consider emotionally weak or vulnerable. Bullies imperviously ignore protests, often responding, "Too bad if you don't like it; take it or leave it."

You may wonder if the bully feels bad about hurting and exploiting others. The answer is no. Bullies have a conscience with as many holes as a thin slice of Swiss cheese. Counter a bully and you'll hear the bully respond, "I'm going to make you regret you ever met me." In contrast to those who practice the golden rule and treat others as well as or better than they treat themselves, bullies seek to rule.

Bullies do, however, protect those they see as important to, or as extensions of, themselves. Thus, many bully parents dote on their children yet trash their spouses. In the work world, bullies care about those who gratify their egos or can help them succeed, often showing one face to those higher in the organizational hierarchy and another to peers or subordinates.

Bullies hate seeing others receive more rewards, demonstrate greater talent, or achieve better success. While truly self-confident individuals don't need to put others down to feel big, bullies' aggressive behaviors are designed to prove to others and themselves that they're superior.

Bullies *need* to win and exert power to dominate emotionally, physically, and psychologically as well as to win workplace rewards. They consider the workplace a pecking order and endlessly work to prove they're the biggest rooster.

You may ask, "What's the difference between bullies and other difficult workplace personalities?" Many people can be difficult or unpleasant, particularly if others give them reason. For example, you may work with someone who occasionally lashes out at you, particularly when under stress. This person may not intend to snap at you and may even apologize for it. In contrast, bullies knowingly and *persistently* intimidate, humiliate, and threaten others, without remorse.

ALL BULLIES ARE NOT ALIKE

While bullies don't wear black hats, you can train yourself to recognize the seven classic workplace bully types. Which of these have you encountered in your work life?

The Angry, Aggressive Jerk

You may have met a bully like Bernard, the shouting want-to-be drill sergeant boss who stomped and stormed with self-righteous anger. Bernard's favorite tactic when a new employee joined the group was to announce a discussion topic at staff meetings and then shout, "Speak! Ideas! Cream rises to the top. This is your chance to shine and keep your job!" When a brave new employee offered a suggestion, Bernard yelled, "Wrong answer!" and as the new employee looked around in dismay, "You're fired." New employees who took the bait and got up to leave the room then heard Bernard's manic laughter as he enjoyed his joke.

Perhaps you work alongside an outspoken, fault-finding coworker like Camille, who demands you play the passive, obedient listener as she bashes others. The moment you protest by defending the coworker who has landed on Camille's bad side, Camille turns her fury on you. If you "learn your lesson," you no longer voice ideas contrary to Camille's, but instead listen mutely to her monologue.

Not always right but never in doubt, the angry, aggressive bully gets right in your face and tells you off when he's having a bad day. These arrogant know-it-alls mask incompetence with bombast and act as if everyone else is a lesser being. Wielding nitpicking comments as weapons, they erode the self-esteem of those around them.

Here's what you can expect when you work around an angry, aggressive jerk:

- Blaming, demeaning, belittling comments
- Insults and name-calling
- Fault-finding and harangues about your incompetence

Working around an angry, aggressive jerk keeps you on constant emotional and physical high-alert since the next attack may come any minute. This tension saps your energy, leaving you increasingly less able to handle the continued onslaught.

In Chapters 7, 9, 10, and 12 you'll find strategies for silencing the angry, aggressive jerk.

The Scorched-Earth Fighter

MARIE AND WAYNE initially went into business together but soon found they couldn't work well together. When they first met, Wayne liked Marie for her personal strength and talents; he soon hated her for the small ways in which she stood up to him. When others complimented Marie for her talent and accomplishments, Wayne burned inside. In his world, Wayne intended to reign as king with no queen, only loyal subjects.

Marie didn't mind Wayne taking the lead in most areas, but she had a brain. Although she never argued, she voiced her opinions. This was too much for Wayne; he didn't want others having views different from his. He thundered his disapproval whenever Marie asked him to consider an alternative.

Marie watched as employees who sided with her cast their eyes down when Wayne slammed his fist in anger on her desk. She worried that Wayne would take his anger at her out on them. Her supporters shared Marie's concern, and one by one they joined Wayne's camp, quit, or were fired by Wayne when Marie was off-site with clients.

After several months, Marie realized she was becoming someone she didn't want to be, her fear clinging to her like sweat. She stopped voicing her opinions. "Yes, Wayne, whatever you decide" became her mantra. When she heard her own voice, she didn't recognize the plaintive tone.

Still, Marie stayed, hoping things would change. One day, she caught sight of her image in the restroom mirror and didn't immediately recognize herself. Her head hung low, her shoulders were stooped, and her eyes had lost their sparkle. Was she a role model for her employees, or a picture of what not to become?

When Marie finally told Wayne she needed to dissolve their partnership, she no longer saw herself as someone deserving of respect. She left Wayne everything, from her cell phone to all the products, services, and systems they'd built during their three-year partnership.

Wayne wasn't done with Marie. He hated her for leaving and denounced her to everyone who would listen. He made it clear to his employees that if they connected with Marie in any way, it was an act of disloyalty to him. Wayne needed to win.

Because Wayne was so sure of himself, he was convincing. Soon, most employees agreed with him that any past problems stemmed from Marie's poor judgment. Others in the industry also took sides, few remembering Marie's talents and most believing Wayne's pronouncements. Marie didn't have enough faith in herself left to stay in the industry in which she'd formerly excelled. She chose a new field and began the long, slow climb back to the person she had been.

The so-convinced-he's-right, "scorched-earth" fighter pulls out all the stops to take out his opponent. Wayne, willing to do anything and everything to win, typifies this cold, calculating, cutthroat, bully type.

It wasn't enough for Wayne to win; he needed anyone who crossed him to lose. Scorched-earth fighters want everything their targets possess—reputation, authority, connections—and don't stop until they've destroyed anyone who stands up to them.

Chapter 13 contains winning strategies for pouring water on the scorched-earth fighter.

The Silent Grenade

IMPULSIVE, VOLATILE MIKE instilled fear and dread in his peers and employees with unexpected explosions. New employees quickly learned the whispered "storm ahead" warning from a passing coworker meant "stay out of Mike's way; he's in a mood." One icy glance from Mike silenced even the most outspoken.

Mike didn't blow up every day, and this made his outbursts more difficult. His coworkers would get used to the calm Mike and start to feel secure. Then, they'd make a casual comment and watch in horror as Mike's jaw tightened and eyes darkened, signaling an impending eruption. Eventually, they found it easier to avoid casual comments.

"You get used to it," Mike's longer-term employees told the new hires. "It's sort of like living in a prison camp. Don't get on the warden's radar and you'll do fine." Few employees lasted more than a year.

Silent grenades rule many individuals, and even entire workplaces, because employees, coworkers, and supervisors fear these bullies will fly into an unstoppable rage. Stories abound of how one of these tyrants pounded his fist through a wall or shook a peer so hard his teeth rattled. Grenades destroy others' morale and job satisfaction by threatening impending tirades.

Chapter 14 presents strategies for defusing the silent grenade.

The Shape-Shifter

CAREN TYPIFIES the shape-shifter bully. A charismatic, talented individual, Caren quickly impressed her new boss, who didn't realize she'd hired an opportunistic, manipulative backstabber until it was almost too late.

Caren's coworkers experienced her duplicity almost immediately. "Girl, don't mess with me," Caren told Angelica when Angelica tried to show her how to correctly save her files on the server.

"I was just trying to help you learn our systems," said Angelica in surprise.

"You stay out of my way and things will be just fine," Caren snapped, and Angelica retreated.

When Angelica went to the boss with her concerns, she was told "I'm sure Caren didn't mean what you thought; she's just trying to learn on her own. This cattiness is beneath you. I expect you to help her." As Angelica left her boss's office, she almost bumped into Caren, who flashed a smug smile.

"Caren, I can't finish the team's marketing report until I get your section," Tom said with a friendly smile as he stopped by Caren's office.

"I didn't know I was supposed to write anything," countered Caren.

"It's what I outlined to you yesterday," said a puzzled Tom.

"I can't do what you don't tell me," barked Caren in an irritated voice.

"If you have a minute, I'll go over it again."

"I don't have time," answered Caren flatly, turning back to her computer screen.

Tom opened his mouth, shut it, and left. He didn't mention anything to their boss. When he submitted the report, the boss asked why he'd left out Caren's section. "I wasn't able to get it from her," answered Tom.

"But Tom, she gave me her draft yesterday. Next time, ask her," scolded his boss. Not sure how to tell the boss he'd tried without looking like a fool, Tom left, his worries unspoken.

Always flattering to your face if you're the boss, the shape-shifter plays the charmer to those from whom she seeks opportunities and of whom she intends to take advantage. These chameleon-like bullies float through the workplace on power granted them by supervisors who see only their fawning facade.

Those whom a shape-shifter views as beneath her, or from whom she can gain nothing, soon feel her claws. When these coworkers call the shape-shifter on her two-faced behavior, she responds with protesting words that contradict her knowing eyes as she gives them a "Cross me if you dare, I can take you out" smirk.

One by one, shape-shifter bullies establish their status in the office pecking order even as they weaken their coworkers' relationships with the boss. By acting the model employee and pretending coworkers misjudge or mistreat them, they successfully garner the boss's protection.

Although the boss finally caught on and fired Caren, the damage had been done as Tom, Angelica, and others of her victims lost respect for their boss.

Chapter 15 presents strategies on seeing through the shape-shifter.

The Narcissist Manipulator

IT WASN'T ENOUGH for Pauline that she'd been hired into a senior position; she set out to destroy head nurse Molly, the other senior manager. Not only did Molly's anguish not matter to Pauline, she didn't even notice it. When the managing physician fired Pauline, he told her that he held her responsible for driving Molly away. Pauline insisted she hadn't: "Molly *chose* to resign." And she believed it!

Narcissist bullies see the world through a lens of "me, only me" and feel they're inherently superior to others. They feel entitled to win every contest, play by their own rules, and don't mind making others look stupid. Although they pursue their own needs without regard for the impact on others or their organizations, they rapidly rise through the ranks because they excel at selling themselves.

Behavioral and nonverbal clues reveal the narcissist bully. They strut like peacocks with unfurled tail feathers. They make eye contact as if they've learned the technique but not the art. Preoccupied with themselves and their ambitions, they lack empathy and when you talk to them about your or others' feelings, your words fall on deaf ears. They resist any criticism; instead, they project their own flaws onto others.

Do narcissist bullies regret stomping on your rights? No, you got in their way and if you didn't want to be trampled, you would have been more careful. Narcissists break rules when doing so serves their purpose, without worrying about the normal rules of decent behavior. If the narcissist bully hurts your feelings when she arrogantly devalues you, does she notice? No, she considers it your problem that you're so easily offended.

In Chapter 16, I've outlined strategies for handling the narcissist bully.

Wounded Rhino: Malevolent and Powerful

TECHNOLOGY MANAGER JACK, a large man at six foot three inches tall and 290 pounds, ruled the nonprofit where he worked. When he was displeased, his jaw thrust forward and he bellowed.

If you fell out of favor with Jack, things happened. Computer gremlins surfaced. Files went missing. Your maintenance or IT request went to the bottom of the queue or disappeared. No one ever accused Jack of sabotage—it wasn't worth it.

If you asked Jack's peers when they expected action after they put in an IT request, they'd say, "Jack time." Even the executive director backed down when Jack hollered, "You'll have it when I get to it" if she reminded him a certain report was due. Jack never responded to Outlook staff meeting requests. Still, the executive director couldn't help asking, "Are you going to make the staff meeting?" if she ran into Jack in the hall. "Don't have time," he always said.

No one questioned Jack's effectiveness; things ran smoothly—unless someone ticked him off. "He's a dragon, but I don't know what we'd do without him," said the executive director. "He knows our computer system and equipment inside and out. We couldn't afford to replace Jack's skills if he ever decided to leave."

Although the nonprofit's accounting manager, Lexie, stayed out of Jack's way, she didn't fear him. When Jack hollered, she looked amused. When she had computer issues, she called her computer technician son and had him fix them. If you asked Lexie why she paid for repairs out of her own pocket, she said simply, "My son needs the money and I'm not knuckling under."

When the executive director announced her plan to retire, employees expected the board to select Lexie as the next executive director at the upcoming meeting and looked forward to her promotion. Employees liked her firm, straightforward approach.

Fearing some staff members might resign, the executive director didn't tell employees that Jack had also applied for the promotion. Jack didn't mention it either; he figured he'd be chosen. Jack didn't know that a board member had privately called each manager and senior staff member except Lexie and Jack and said, "Please keep this call confidential. We have some external candidates, but I would like to know if any current managers would make a good executive director."

Three days before the board meeting, Lexie discovered a rogue virus had wiped out accounting records. "Can't be fixed," said Jack. Lexie called her son and then an outside service who confirmed Jack's diagnosis.

"Thank God for last week's backup," Lexie thought, only to discover that the backup tape was also compromised. Lexie suspected Jack had engineered her problems. Lexie and her team pulled two all-nighters, re-creating as much of the work as they could using paper records to update the prior month's backup.

As accounting manager, Lexie routinely provided the board members a quarterly financial review and had also planned to brief them on the fund-raising efforts she'd spearheaded. Exhausted, Lexie presented an abbreviated version of the review and briefing and explained there had been a computer malfunction.

"Just a darn minute," Jack leapt up from his seat at the rear of the boardroom. "Don't go blaming IT for slipshod management. We can't fix stupid."

"What do you mean, Jack?" asked a board member known to be Jack's drinking buddy.

Jack preened. "While IT has antivirus software and protocols to prevent viruses, we can't prevent human error. Someone on the accounting team intentionally disabled our preventative measures to be able to download a corrupted application and that brought down the accounting department."

"He just implied I run a loose ship," thought Lexie. "How clever. If I can't run accounting, how could I possibly oversee the whole operation?"

Perhaps the scariest bullies are the authoritarian, forceful, mean-spirited individuals who dominate and control others' work lives. These bullies attack with vengeance and without qualms. Like the scorched-earth fighters, wounded rhinos battle ruthlessly; however, they seek domination rather than destruction of their target.

Like the animal from which they get their name, wounded rhinos are ill-tempered and become more so when they're disturbed. When attacking, a real rhino lowers its head, snorts, breaks into a gallop reaching thirty miles or more an hour, and gores or strikes powerful blows with its horns.

You may feel a calculated malevolence exuding from the wounded rhino in your workplace. These bullies delight in your squirming and deliberately undermine you in an attempt to feel superior. Wounded rhinos run rampant over those they perceive are in their way, regardless of the consequences; they simply don't care.

Chapter 17 offers you strategies for avoiding the wounded rhino's charge.

The Character Assassin

"A REAL BITCH," Kevin said, talking behind closed doors with each of his coworkers about his supervisor, Georgia. Kevin regaled each listener with detailed stories, some true but most made up, concerning Georgia's foibles. When Georgia irritated a fellow employee, Kevin lost no time making sure every staff member knew all the details, presented one-sidedly and with embellishment.

Kevin beat a path to each newly hired employee's desk. "Just for your own protection," he told them, "don't trust Georgia. She's responsible for a lot of heartache. You need to know she secretly tapes meetings with you, reads your emails, and listens in on your calls."

Some of the employees whom Kevin warned quit before the end of their first day. Others distrusted whatever Georgia told them about her management style. Oddly, none distrusted Kevin. Thus, Kevin successfully trashed his target's reputation.

Kevin spent hours on the Internet, researching Georgia and setting up alternate Hotmail, Facebook, and Yahoo accounts from which he posted nasty remarks and bogus stories about her. Kevin never worried about the truth, only about creating stories that would titillate those who viewed his posts.

While Georgia never discovered who initiated the horrid posts, she knew it had to be someone with whom she worked. Eventually she quit and moved to a different state.

Character assassins tell destructive stories about others to discredit them and get them out of the way. They ruthlessly defame their targets and knock others down so they can feel taller. They act without remorse and enjoy the results they achieve.

Chapter 18 contains strategies for neutralizing the character assassin's reputation damage.

Chances are you've met a few of these seven bully types, including some who combine elements of several types. They lurk in every workplace, and unless you learn to handle yourself, you're prey.

The good news starts with the next chapter.

Your Turn: Where Are You Now?

1. Which of these bully types have you met, or is your bully a combination of several of these types? What can you add to the descriptions in this chapter?
2. What does a bully's lack of internal brakes tell you about what you can and can't expect when you next encounter a bully?
3. Have you met a bully who rationalized his or her behavior? If you haven't, imagine what it might be like. If you initially believed the bully's excuses and later realized you'd let that bully evade responsibility, what would you like to say to this bully now?
4. Select a bully currently in your work life or one you've recently encountered. Knowing what you know now, what would you like to say to him or her?
5. What aspects of yourself do you see in those on the receiving end of bullying in these anecdotes? How can you use one or more of these real-life stories to create a starting point from which you can address your own situation more effectively than you otherwise might have?
6. Which bully type do you fear the most? How come?
7. How has a bully demeaned, threatened, or intimidated you?
8. Do you feel bullies have remorse? What does your answer tell you?
9. What should you do if you work under a Bernard or alongside a Camille?

10. What do you wish Marie had done?
11. Who do think eventually succeeded, Jack or Lexie?
12. How have you been demeaned or threatened by a bully?
13. What's the best insight you've gained from this chapter?
14. What's one step you'll put into place that's within your expanding comfort zone and doesn't pose a risk to you? Whatever step you select, take it within seven days.

IT'S YOUR CHOICE: TO CONFRONT OR NOT TO CONFRONT

We must build dikes of courage to hold back the flood of fear.

—MARTIN LUTHER KING JR.

LIKE MANY BULLIES, WAYNE sought out a new victim after Marie fled their partnership. He zeroed in on Arnold.

"Hey, little man, what kind of crap is this?" Wayne challenged when Arnold handed him a report at the end of the morning meeting. Arnold felt, more than saw, his coworkers cast their eyes to the ground and slink away. He'd seen this happen when Wayne had "poked fun" at Marie. Heck, he'd slunk away himself.

What to do? He couldn't think of a thing to say. Perhaps accommodation was the safest route. "I'll take it back and fix it."

"You do that, little man," Wayne mocked. "And don't bring me crap again."

Four hours later, Arnold called his wife and said, "I'll be home late. I've got to rework the project."

"What? You slaved over that for weeks. You were so proud of it when you finished yesterday."

"Well, the boss didn't like it."

After he hung up the phone, Arnold looked at his work and ran through ways to defend it if Wayne rejected it again.

"No magic bullet," he thought. I'll create a new cover page; that's all Wayne glanced at before tossing it back to me. It's that or get a new job.

SEVEN STEPS TO CONFRONTING CONFRONTATION

If you face a Wayne, a bully who continually provokes you, here's what works.

Step #1: Control Your Initial Reaction

Imagine a large, angry tiger leaping toward you, its teeth bared in a ferocious snarl. If you truly imagine this, you may feel your breath catching, back stiffening, and the urge to run. In the grip of your desire to flee, you lose the battle before it begins. The tiger, able to outrun you, sinks its claws and teeth into your back.

When you react to a threat, you rarely think clearly and sometimes don't think at all. If, like most people, your reaction is one of fear, you may temporarily stop breathing or breathe shallowly and rapidly. When that happens, you momentarily lose easy, simultaneous access to both mental hemispheres, the left and the right.

Fear caused by the bully's intimidation "pulls" you toward processing information in your right hemisphere, the hemisphere that comes into play when you emotionally react, develop creative approaches, or access your intuition.

To handle bullying, you also need the ability to think and to put your thoughts into language. These functions, along with the ability to strategize and think ahead to future consequences, are located in your left hemisphere.

Table 5-1 outlines the mental functions of the left and right hemispheres.

This explains why you may occasionally be unable to speak when upset, or say things you later regret deeply. It also explains why you can realize so much intuitively, yet not be able to use what you perceive in an analytical, problem-solving manner.

LEFT HEMISPHERE	RIGHT HEMISPHERE
Logic	Reaction
Analysis and problem solving	Emotion
Language	Intuition
Sense of future consequences	Creativity

Table 5-1. Brain function: The role of the left and right hemispheres.

If you are able to calm yourself by slowing and deepening your breathing, you increase your ability to access left and right hemispheres simultaneously and to couple analysis and problem-solving with emotion, intuition, and creativity.

The Coastline Breathing Technique. To quickly and successfully learn to slow your breathing, try "coastline breathing."

Here's how: Imagine you're standing on a beach. Let yourself watch the waves moving first toward, and then away from, the shore. Does the image of watching waves calm you? If you find the sensation of watching waves relaxing, you're halfway to learning coastline breathing.

Now, notice your breathing as air moves in and out of your nose and chest. Breathing flows like waves; there's an inhalation, a transitional pause, an exhalation, and another transitional pause. In coastline breathing, you notice your breathing rhythm in the same way you might watch waves.

Close your eyes and try it. As you focus on your breathing as air flows in and out of your nose and chest, you'll notice the rhythm automatically slows and deepens. Once you can allow your breathing to slow and deepen with your eyes closed, open your eyes and see if you can slow and deepen your breathing simply by paying attention to it.

Test this out, and allow yourself to slowly breathe while you pay attention to something else, such as the words in this book. You've learned coastline breathing, an essential step in controlling your initial reaction, so the bully no longer takes control of you or the situation.

Step #2: Control Your Response

Controlling your initial instinctive reaction frees you to respond rather than react and leaves you free to choose whether and how to handle a bully. While you may feel trapped or intimidated by the situation the bully has put you in, you have choices; you simply have to uncover them.

Step #3: Assess the Situation

Controlling your response and assessing the situation creatively helps you make a set of choices you'll feel comfortable with and lays the foundation for developing your mental game plan. Ask yourself:

- What's going on?
- Is this how I want to be treated?
- Is this situation or bully worth taking on?
- If so, how?

Before you act, make a detailed assessment of what's going on. In this way, you'll be able to develop the right plan as well as the confidence you need to put your plan into action.

Before Acting, Questions to Ask Yourself. Imagine that I'm sitting across the table from you and asking you the following questions. It may help to answer them out loud as if I'm right there, or to write out your answers on paper or on your computer. If you prefer, you can simply think through the answers.

1. Describe your bully. Is she new to your organization or a long-term employee? What role does she play in your work life? Is she your boss, a coworker, or another employee?
2. What do you depend on the bully for and how does the bully depend on you? (Although the bully may frustrate you by not giving you the answers you need to finish projects, if the bully depends on you for information or other assistance, you have leverage.)
3. How do others see your bully? Do they see her as a bully or simply as a strong-willed, opinionated individual? What does she bring to the organization in terms of talents?
4. Where and when does the bully hassle you—behind closed doors or in front of an audience?
5. Was the bullying a one-time incident or is it ongoing?
6. How does she bully you; that is, what does she actually do? Is it the words she uses, her tone of voice, or the look on her face? (Pick one or two instances and describe them in detail.)
7. How is the bully's behavior affecting you?
8. Have you told the bully the situation needs to change?

Step #4: Determine Why You Are the Target

Next, ask yourself "Why me?" not to blame yourself, which you may have done in the past, but to try to figure out what led this particular bully to select you.

Before Acting, Questions to Ask Yourself. Ask yourself the following questions:

1. Were you simply in the wrong place at the wrong time, or did you ignore warning signs and stay in a situation you should have left? Does the bully want something you have, whether it's your job or relationships? Does the bully mea-

sure himself against you in some way, and because you're older, younger, prettier, smarter, thinner, married, single, aligned with the boss, more popular, or more skilled, consider you a threat to his position or to getting what he wants?

2. Does the bully underestimate you, your resiliency, or your ability to stand up for yourself? If so, how have you contributed to this? Have you signaled you're an easy target or put up with crappy treatment? Have you given away your power?
3. Does your bully think you lack alliances and thus doesn't worry about others coming to your aid? If so, perhaps you can fight back without fighting the bully directly, by developing your relationships with others. Intriguingly, we don't always need to fight the villains in our lives; we simply have to improve our lives. Thus, a bullying incident can be a wake-up call letting us know we need to make positive changes.
4. Does this person single you out, or is he an equal-opportunity problem to everyone? If he bullies others, you may be able to enlist them if you decide to take further action.

Step #5: Analyze the Pros and Cons of Taking on the Bully

Before you go on to the next part of the assessment, how are you feeling? By putting a name to any negative emotions, you start to process them. You may also find that writing out or speaking your answers aloud ignites your determination to handle the bully.

Before Acting, Questions to Ask Yourself. Now, decide what you want to do about the situation. Ask yourself a series of questions.

1. Is this how you want to be treated? This may be the simplest part of your assessment. If your answer is "no," say it mentally or out loud in a strong, firm voice: "**No**."

2. Is this bully or situation worth taking on? You don't need to tackle every bully or situation. Some people and situations won't change even if you handle the situation effectively. Understanding and accepting this reality and moving on, rather than letting yourself be mowed down, may be the strongest move you could make.

   Sometimes, it feels right to exit the situation. If you decide you're not ready for the fight, or if the eventual gain isn't worth the battle, you might decide the personal cost or consequences make this an effort you'd rather not launch.
3. What will happen if you do nothing? Can you live with yourself if you don't speak up? What do you intend to achieve by confronting your bully? What are the risks you take and the potential negative outcomes if you confront your bully? Are you willing to suffer those consequences?

   If you take on this fight, will you be able to impact the situation favorably? What resources (time, money, emotional toll, legal fees, brainpower, or energy) will you need to win your battle?

If you *choose* not to tackle a bully or situation, take pride in your choice. You didn't simply give up, you *chose* to not act.

Step #6: Take Back Your Power

More often, however, you'll decide it's worthwhile to take on the bully. Perhaps you love everything about your job except how the bully interferes with your work life. Possibly you've come to a point in your life where you feel you owe it to yourself to take a stand instead of allowing bullying to erode your self-esteem or job satisfaction.

As you'll learn in Chapters 7 and 9, bullies test to see which potential targets might be easy prey. If you initially allow bullying, you encourage repeat, escalated bullying. Further, multiple bully attacks weaken your defenses and impact how others view you. For this reason, if you're wondering whether now or later is the time, now's the time. It makes sense.

An "it's worth it" decision pays off in many ways. First, you feel good about yourself when you take a stand, even if you aren't victorious. Second, you discourage escalated bullying. Third, you may succeed, and the bully may move on or simply stop messing with you. Fourth, each time you tackle a bully, you exercise skills and strategies that strengthen your mental and emotional anti-bully muscles.

Everyone in any workplace has personal power, whether or not they know it or use it. Targets give up their power to the bully. Learn to take back your power by changing how you signal you're "prey." Taking back your power begins inside you and radiates externally in terms of your visible reaction. As a quick experiment, think of a bully you've met or currently deal with. If you don't have one, imagine that you work for or around Wayne and he's taunting you. How do you react? Do you become tense, feel powerless or perhaps angry? What happened to your breathing? If your breathing became rapid and shallow, use the coastline breathing technique and notice the difference it makes. This experiment serves as a brief reminder that everything starts with you and your decision to change and take action.

You have the power to stay with or leave your job. You may feel you have to stay in your current job; however, that's your choice. If you leave, others in your current workplace lose what you bring to the table. It's your choice; you have the power to take your talents with you.

Step #7: Decide on Your Game Plan

In this final assessment step, "if so, how," you decide on your game plan. (You'll learn a variety of strategies, and the skills you need to carry them out, in Chapters 7 through 20.) Now, we'll examine ways to build your confidence, so that you can carry out any strategy you choose.

The act of stopping a bully starts with you.

CONFIDENCE-BUILDING TECHNIQUES

Imagine a friend asks you to walk the length of a two-by-four plank laid on the ground. No doubt you could walk the full length. Now imagine the same friend says she'll pay you $10 if you'll walk the plank's length again, only now she moves it three inches off the ground. Chances are you'll smile and do it. Now imagine she raises it ten feet off the ground and offers you $100 to walk its full length. Would you walk the plank you've walked twice before or hesitate, psyched out by the fear of falling?

Mind Power

Now let's try an experiment designed to show you the power of your mind. Please stand, taking the book with you, and notice where your feet are. You'll leave your feet in the same position in both phases of this exercise. Now turn your entire body, without moving your feet, to either the right or left side and look at the furthest spot on the wall you can see comfortably.

Without sitting down, turn back so that you're again facing forward. Leaving your feet in the same position as earlier, imagine that a cloud of empowering, relaxing light descends around your head. Allow yourself to feel this relaxing energy massaging the back and sides of your head and neck. Let yourself feel your neck becoming more supple, flexible, and malleable.

Imagine the empowering and relaxing energy continues to descend. It now massages your shoulders and the upper ribs of your back. Allow yourself to feel your back and shoulders becoming looser, more at ease, and much more relaxed. Imagine the light massaging your entire back. Allow your back to continue feeling more relaxed, supple, limber, and at ease. Now, with your feet in the same place as earlier, turn your entire body, except for your feet, and notice the furthest spot on the wall you can see comfortably. How much farther do you see? You've just experienced the power of your mind.

Mental Martial Arts

There's more. You're about to learn how to use mental martial arts to strengthen your inner self. When we give mental ground to the aggressor coming toward us, we weaken. Instead, you can use the power of visualization to center yourself, so you don't react. Here's why and how this works:

We process information in three ways: visually (by seeing), auditorily (by hearing), and kinesthetically (by feeling and through physical sensation).

Auditory processing, which we use in verbal confrontation, moves at the speed of sound, roughly 80 to 180 words a minute. When you listen to another's words and fully absorb them, you think or process information at a rate of 80 to 180 words per minute. If you mentally dialogue with yourself when another person talks, as in "Why am I letting this guy do this?" you often miss part of what the speaker says because your mental dialogue processes at the same 80 to 180 words minute.

Kinesthetic or emotional and physical processing moves more slowly than speech, slower than 80 words per minute. Thus, when we get upset, we can't always keep up with conversations.

In contrast, visual processing moves at the speed of light, the equivalent of 900 to 1,400 words per minute. You can use this difference in processing speed to steady yourself in a confrontation, or when you're nervous or upset. Because the slowest visual processing (900 words per minute) moves more quickly than the fastest auditory processing (180 words per minute), if you flash on an image in your mind even as you hear the other person talking, the image can calm you or "ground you," while still allowing you to hear the person's words.

To see how it works, try this: Close your eyes and see one of your children or your pet in an adorable moment. Or imagine the face of someone you love or a scene in nature such as a waterfall, a beach, or a sailboat floating calmly on the sea.

Now open your eyes and look at whatever surrounds you, and, at the same time—without closing your eyes—mentally flash on the image you've created. "Flash" means you don't become fully absorbed in what you mentally picture; instead, you momentarily see the image even as you remain fully aware of what's going on around you. You can do this once or several times as you're concurrently paying attention to what's happening outside you.

Once you get the hang of mental multitasking, turn on the radio or television and notice that you can hear the words a disk jockey or television personality is speaking while simultaneously mentally flashing on an image in your mind. Flashing on the visual image allows you to feel centered without missing another person's words. You can even flash on an image while *you're* talking. Try it.

You've now achieved alternate focus, a key step in mental martial arts. By grounding yourself through alternative focus, you come from a centered frame of reference when confronting the bully. No longer do you give full mental control to what the bully says.

You can use this same technique, with other images, to strengthen yourself. Imagine Katharine Hepburn with her head held high, or a majestic mountain such as Mount Everest. Do your neck and back straighten as you think of Katharine? Does focusing, in the back of your mind, on Mount Everest give you a sense of strength?

Now contrast what happens when you visualize an image that centers you with what happens to you when you are confronted and don't use this strategy. When you're confronted or feel threatened, intimidated, anxious, or powerless, you process kinesthetically, at less than 80 words a minute. Confrontation and intimidation can literally dumb you down.

As I've demonstrated, it doesn't have to. You can control your reaction with these easy-to-learn strategies. To review:

1. **Breathe:** So you can simultaneously access both the left and right hemispheres of your brain and add analysis and problem solving to your emotional and intuitive processing.
2. **Assess:** Consider what's going on; is this how you want to be treated? Is this situation or bully worth taking on? If so, how?
3. **Visualize:** Develop an internal alternate focus by seeing an image that calms you even as you listen to the other person speak.

Your Turn: Where Are You Now?

1. Make coastline breathing a habit. Starting now, commit to practicing coastline breathing at least three times a day.

   Once you find you can easily slow your breathing, commit to using coastline breathing whenever a situation or person takes you by surprise or upsets you. Once coastline breathing becomes a habit, you'll have more control over many situations.
2. What are the benefits for you of coastline breathing? How does it make you feel (more relaxed, floating . . .)?
3. Create two powerful images that help you center yourself, and practice visualizing them while listening to others and while you yourself are talking. How does it feel? You might want to create several images: one that relaxes you, another that empowers you, and perhaps another that

reminds you how supported you are by God or those who love you.

4. If you haven't yet done so, ask yourself the assessment questions. If this proves stressful, you might want to engage a coach to partner with you as you do the assessment. You may also find coastline breathing and visualization helpful. Do any of your answers surprise you? If so, what is surprising? How do your answers help you break the situation down into manageable pieces?
5. Has your assessment helped you arrive at a decision, or does it better enable you to seek another person's support or help?
6. Thinking through situations, even ones you didn't successfully handle, helps you plan how you will deal with future situations. Commit to regular assessment as you move through *Beating the Workplace Bully,* adjusting for the new strategies you learn and the successes you achieve.
7. When you learn to control yourself, you learn to control situations and are no longer a victim. You have to be in control to create control. It starts with you. For the next week, breathe when anything challenging, frustrating, or intimidating happens.

   Notice what happens to you when you breathe, and ask yourself, "What are my options?" Whatever option you choose, you've now become the one who chooses.

PUT ON YOUR GAME FACE: DON'T PLAY BY THE BULLY'S RULES

I learned that courage was not the absence of fear, but the triumph over it. The brave man is not he who does not feel afraid, but he who conquers that fear.

—NELSON MANDELA

ONLY ONE THING STOOD in the way of Todd getting the promotion he wanted: Floyd.

The two men couldn't have been more different. Todd, a self-righteously arrogant man, barked orders at his employees, and they performed for him. Floyd, a quiet, unassuming individual, earned his employees' respect by doing his job and giving them credit. When Floyd's company made the decision to purchase Todd's, everyone knew that after the merger became complete, one of the two men would receive the title of department director and the other would be demoted from department manager to a line supervisor position.

In the five months prior to the merger becoming complete, the men frequently sat in the same meetings. Todd seized every opportunity to rattle Floyd. When he learned that Floyd felt self-conscious about his turkey wattle, he stared at Floyd's neck. When the chief executive officer asked Todd and Floyd, along with other managers, to meet with their counterparts and plan how to create efficiencies as they merged departments, Todd scoffed, "That's what you think works?" when Floyd offered his ideas.

Todd's bullying worked. Floyd began to stammer, both in Todd's presence and when asked to put forth ideas at managers' meetings. Increasingly, he sat mute. When the senior managers met to choose which of the former managers to promote to director, they selected Todd. "Floyd's a great guy," said one, "but he doesn't handle change well. This merger has completely rattled him."

Bullies set games in motion and win if we play their games. If you want to escape a bully's control, you need to put on your game face, and then change the game.

PUT ON YOUR GAME FACE

Whoever said "fake it till you make it" spoke wisely. Here's a quick experiment that may surprise you. Stand or sit as if you're depressed. Your head goes down, your shoulders slump, and your chest bows inward. Now, maintain that stance while thinking "confidence, energy, enthusiasm, and power." If you're like most people, these positive words make you want to straighten up.

Now, stand as if you just won the Publishers Clearing House's million-dollar prize. Chances are that your demeanor changed to one of exuberance and excitement. Now, allow yourself to feel intimidated, fearful, humiliated, or depressed and, at the same time, try to maintain that joyous stance. Did you find it hard to do?

That's the impact of how you feel on how you look. How you feel impacts how you physically stand or sit and how you stand or sit impacts what you feel. The good news is you can learn how to put on a game face and simultaneously make yourself feel more confident.

LOOK AT YOURSELF FROM THE OUTSIDE IN

When a bully confronts you, do you quake inside? Or visibly telegraph that you're intimidated by trembling or reddening? Do you show your fear by breathing rapidly and shallowly? Bullies watch body language and pounce when they detect hesitancy.

What if instead of trembling and breathing faster, you took a calming breath, visualized an image that gave you a sense of strength, and then stood or sat tall with your head up, chin out, and eyes focused on what was in front of you? Not only would you send an "I'm not the easy prey you think" nonverbal message, your stance would have a positive effect on how you felt *inside*, where you most needed it.

Let's try another experiment. Sit like a lady (even you guys), ankles crossed, hands folded in your lap. Could you possibly take up any less space? Do you feel submissive in that position? You do the same thing to yourself when you fear a bully's attack and sit slouched with your eyes averted, shoulders slumped, chest caved in, and head down. In other words, you increase your feeling of surrender.

Now sit like a confident, secure, assertive individual, and you'll notice that you immediately take up more space even though your body size doesn't actually change.

How do you stand when you are nervous or feel intimidated? Slouched to the side or erect as a strong, assertive, confident person would? Try this experiment. Stand erect, legs apart, head up, eyes open, chin out, and your weight balanced equally on both feet. Notice how it feels. Then slouch to the left or right, lower your head, and hunch your shoulders. In which position do you feel stronger?

Take a few minutes to practice sitting tall while you breathe deeply and slowly. You can read while you do this. How does this posture make you feel? If you're like most of us, physically sitting or standing erect and thus acting "as if" you feel confident both strengthens you from the outside in and sends a message to the bully and others.

Let's add additional armor. Just as in the last chapter, you thought of a loved one, child, pet, or nature scene to ground yourself, visualize an image that gives you strength—perhaps someone you love, a cherished grandparent, someone who symbolizes bravery, or a mountain range. Now, focus on this image as you sit or stand erect.

Once you have the image in your mind, practice mentally flashing on it while paying full attention to whatever's going on around you at the same time as you adopt a stance or sitting posture that exudes strength and confidence. By mentally multitasking and marshaling your outward appearance, you will learn to act at ease when confronted, even when initially intimidated, by a bully. In this way, you mentally prepare yourself to handle effectively whatever comes and simultaneously send a strong, nonverbal signal to anyone planning to bully or actually bullying you.

REFUSE TO PLAY THE BULLY'S GAME

Do you remain silent when bullied? Bullies pick on people who don't fight back and tread on those, like Sonja and Tova, who allow them to. They count on their ability to intimidate you. They try to control you with demands. They weaken you with demeaning statements.

Remain silent and you collude with bullies. If you kowtow, acquiesce, or "turn the other cheek," hoping to avoid conflict, you may discover that bullies often slap that other cheek. If you want to avoid bully-collusion, you have to speak up in a manner that says, "I stand up to you. I stand up for me." To do otherwise offers bullies a green light.

Make the Rules: Set Limits

A sign outside a coffee shop says, "Unattended children will be given espresso and a free kitten." With that simple statement the coffee shop declares, "Parents, don't let your kids run loose." Similarly, you refuse to play the bully's game when you decide what is right for you, and what you will and won't allow. This means setting boundaries for how you'll let others treat you.

It may be hard for you to set boundaries if you:

- Don't know yourself
- Put others' needs and feelings first
- Fear that setting boundaries might jeopardize relationships you want
- Don't believe you have rights

You can learn to create boundaries by thinking about the work life you want for yourself, then describing this life in terms of what you feel you have the right to expect from others. These statements become your personal "bill of rights."

My Personal Bill of Rights

Here are some sample statements to get you started. You may decide you want to adopt all of them; you may want to add others:

- ☐ I have the right to my own point of view and to express my opinions.
- ☐ I have the right to judge my own behavior, thoughts, and feelings.
- ☐ I have the right to make my own decisions.
- ☐ I have the right to ask for what I want.
- ☐ I have the right to be successful.
- ☐ I have the right to keep my personal life private.
- ☐ I treat others with respect and I deserve to be treated with respect.

What do these boundaries mean?

If you have the right to your own opinions and a workplace bully tells you what to think about coworkers, your supervisor, or situations, you have the right to say, "I don't see it that way." If someone talks over you, you have the right to say what you intended to say after the interrupter finishes. While you generally don't need to interrupt him, don't let his talking over you take away your right to speak. If he does it again, you have the right to say, "Let me finish."

If you have the right to judge your own behavior and you work with a judgmental bully who puts you down, you have the right to assess yourself and counter her criticism or, realizing her negative comments say more about her than they do about you, say nothing.

If you have the right to make your own decisions, and you work alongside someone who persists in deciding for you, you have the right to say, "I don't agree. Here's what I've decided."

If you have the right to ask for what you want, you can ask for respect in all interactions. You have the right, for example, to ask your boss for a raise. If this leads to an insulting discussion that makes you wither, you have the right to look for a job that offers the respect you deserve. Chapters 8, 9, and 20 offer strategies to use when circumstances prevent you from seeking new employment and you work for a boss who persistently treats you less well than you deserve.

If you have the right to be successful and a bully coworker proclaims "You're getting a big head," or "Who do you think you are?" when you shine, you have the right to see jealousy for what it is. Chapter 9 offers novel ways to put jealous snipers in their place.

If you have the right to keep your personal life private, and the bully at your workplace persists in asking personal questions, you have the right to answer, "That's really none of your business."

If you treat others with respect, even when they don't deserve it, it says a great deal about you. It says that respect is one of your core values. Similarly, you absolutely have the right to be treated with respect by everyone in your workplace, whether it's your supervisor, your coworker, or, if you supervise others, your employees. If you decide that respect is an inalienable right and someone treats you poorly, you have the right to say, "I don't allow that."

Warning: Don't violate your own boundaries by:

- Smiling at a joke you find offensive
- Pretending to agree when you disagree
- Going along with a bully who does something you don't like
- Concealing your true feelings
- Pushing yourself or allowing yourself to be pushed beyond your limits
- Allowing disrespect

Set the Rules; End the Game

How does refusing to play the game work and what does it look like in action? When you refuse to play the bully's game, you end the game.

"Don't mind me," your bully says.

"I do mind."

With a single, assertive statement, you change the game.

If the bully yells "Is that all you got done?" at you, you can send your bully a "this far and no further" message by simply answering "Yes" instead of explaining defensively all you did and how long it took.

Can you answer in this way without losing your job if the individual yelling at you is your boss? Let's try it.

Your boss yells at you, "Is that all you got done?"

The response, "Yes, and what would you like me to handle next?" avoids defensiveness yet gives no offense.

When you refuse to play the game the bully sets in motion, you end the game.

Your Turn: Where Are You Now?

1. During the next two days, notice your posture. Are you standing tall? What about when you're confronted by a bully? If you notice yourself shrinking, take a breath; visualize something that gives you power, and stand tall before you speak. Don't wait until you feel strong inside to act strong. This week, practice standing, sitting, and walking strong every day.

   You may find that when you first try this, you overdo it. Don't let that stop you. Learning how to stand and walk strong is like learning to ride a bike. Once you get the hang of it, you'll find it feels increasingly natural; eventually, it becomes second nature.

2. If you haven't yet created an image that gives you a sense of strength or power, create one now. It may help you to consider some of the iconic actresses (Katharine Hepburn, Sandra Bullock, or Barbra Streisand) or actors (Clint Eastwood, John Wayne, or Denzel Washington) who've played strong roles. Or, you could find a picture on the Internet of a mountain peak (Denali, Everest) that symbolizes steadfast strength.

3. Find a mirror and walk toward it. If you were watching you, what would you see as you walked forward? Are your shoulders slumped? Is your chin tucked down? How would you describe your body language if you didn't know you?

   Back up and walk forward again with good posture, your back straight, your shoulders squared, and your head up. Here's a challenge: All week long, practice walking forward with strong strides and your head up, chin out, eyes open, and shoulders back.

4. This week, try an experiment. In at least one situation, pretend to be brave even if you don't feel brave. What changed? How did it feel?

5. Do you have or have you ever had a bully in your work life? If not, imagine what it would be like and answer these questions accordingly. How does your body language change when you're around this person? When you walk into the bully's office or work area, does your head go down, do your shoulders slump? Do you cringe or slightly cower?
6. If you resolved that from this day forward you will project an air of self-confidence, what will you tell yourself to help you accomplish this? How will you change your body language?
7. Create your personal bill of rights. What does each right mean to you?
8. What prevents you from exercising those rights? How will your life be different if you do?
9. Describe one or two situations in which you need to establish boundaries. What boundaries might you establish? How could you express those boundaries creatively (as did the coffeehouse that let parents know unattended children would be given a free kitten)?
10. What makes setting boundaries hard for you?
11. Have you ever violated your own boundaries? If so, where and when? What led you to do so?
12. Have you heard a bully statement recently? If not, make one up. What "game over" response could you have given?
13. If you want further aid in standing tall or marshaling your inner and outer strength, call local martial arts studios. Most give one free lesson, and you may find you love martial arts training.
14. What insights did you get from this chapter? How can you benefit from them?

THE EIGHT MOST COMMON BULLY TRAPS AND HOW TO AVOID THEM

Courage is fire, and bullying is smoke.

—BENJAMIN DISRAELI

LIKABLE ADAM PRIDED HIMSELF on seeing the best in everyone, so when Geoff blasted Adam's ideas for reshaping their department at the staff meeting, Adam thought, "Geoff's having a bad day."

Later, Geoff said in a stage whisper to his sidekick, "Our baby manager's pitiful. Can you believe the garbage that comes out of his mouth?" Adam told himself that Geoff was just having a hard time because Adam had received the promotion Geoff wanted and would come around if given time.

Later that week, as Adam carried two hot, brimful cups of tea back to his desk for another manager and himself, Geoff deliberately bumped into him. "Yeow!" yelped Adam. Geoff guffawed and asked the young receptionist passing them in the hallway, "You hear that cat imitation?" She giggled.

Not knowing what to say, Adam said nothing as he moved off. Adam didn't let his manager know about any of this because (1) he thought he should be able to handle the Geoff situation himself and (2) he feared his manager would think he'd promoted the wrong employee if he couldn't.

If, like Adam, you take the ostrich approach, you signal you're easy prey and give your bully time to gain the upper hand and allow him to take aim at your vulnerabilities.

Bullies lay traps. They thrive on pushing your buttons and making you react. In that way, they lead you to make mistakes that give them the upper hand.

Knowledge is power. In this chapter you will learn how to recognize and avoid these bully traps and, if you fall into one of them, you will learn how to spring up and climb out.

BULLY TRAP #1: DENIAL—PRETENDING WHAT'S HAPPENING ISN'T

Many targets fall into this trap and deny they're being bullied because if they admitted what was happening, they'd have to act. Some people outright deny what's happening. Others minimize, rationalize, or intellectualize what they see and feel. They may even convince themselves that the bully's actions are justified, leaving them with no one to blame but themselves—"I must have done something to provoke this."

If, when you were growing up, someone taught you not to trust your feelings, the lesson you derived was that other people could disregard how you felt. This led you to believe you had no right to protest a bully's taunts. *Bullies love victims who distrust their own feelings.*

Avoid the denial trap. Instead of looking the other way or downplaying the situation, let the bully know by your words and actions, "I see you what you're doing. It stops now." Adam could have moved from doormat to "don't keep messing with me" status by saying, "Geoff, I get that you think you would have been a better choice than I. But you weren't selected. So get over it."

Fear, including worry that his manager might feel he made the wrong choice given Geoff's resistance, prevented Adam from standing up for himself when, in fact, doing so would have reinforced in his manager's mind that he'd chosen well.

Your bully's defeat begins when you admit what's happening and acknowledge the part you play in it. Stop giving bullies the benefit of the doubt. With awareness comes power.

BULLY TRAP #2: COLLUSION—GIVING BULLIES AN OUTPOST IN YOUR HEAD

This was the trap into which Anne fell. She blamed herself for telling Karla things about her personal life that Karla then embellished and spread throughout the office to undermine her. Anne further beat herself up for wanting a friendship with Karla, and told herself that she was "needy." Bullied by Karla, Anne tore at her own self-esteem by criticizing herself for falling prey to a bully's manipulation.

Head nurse Molly wilted under narcissist bully Pauline's relentless "you're not competent" onslaught, and soft-hearted Sonja cowered when Alice verbally abused her. Both Molly and Sonja wondered what they had done wrong to deserve the treatment they received.

You might be mentally calling out "nothing!" on Molly and Sonja's behalf; however, targets often let a bully's words and actions seep into their minds.

Disheartened, Molly retired earlier than she had planned. She let Pauline steal her belief in herself and her pride in twenty years of accomplishment, which included successfully managing both her job and the one Pauline was hired to do. Pauline did a number on Molly, and Molly accepted Pauline's verdict.

Like Molly, Sonja let a bully flatten her self-esteem. When Alice told Sonja "makeup would help" and "heels might make a difference in how your butt looks," Sonja bought new makeup and wore heels to work the next day. Sonja even thanked Alice when she announced "I'm getting you a haircut coupon for Christmas," not realizing until Alice's audience snickered that she'd been set up.

Sonja not only let Alice's words seep into her thoughts, she joined forces with Alice, by beating herself up for allowing the abuse. If instead Sonja had responded "How dare you? Do you need to make yourself feel bigger by taking someone else down?" it would have made a world of difference.

Never collude with a bully by giving the bully an outpost in your mind. A bully's judgmental comments bump into your emotional and mental space in the same way a bully stepping on your foot bumps into your physical space. If you swallow a bully's judgments or allow the bully to shape how you see yourself, you aid and abet the bully. Don't let any bully define who you are. You have the right to judge your own behavior; after all, who knows you better than you do?

In Chapters 8 and 10, you will discover how to develop a tough mental skin, rout the bully from your mind, and develop your fighting spirit.

BULLY TRAP #3: DELUSION—EXPECTING THE BULLY TO CHANGE

MARIE HOPED to work things out with Wayne, thinking that her talent and willingness to let Wayne take the lead in most matters would win him over.

Despite or because of Marie's skills and accomplishments, Wayne wanted her to lose more than he wanted her as a partner. Wayne barked orders at Marie, put her down in front of employees, criticized the quality of her work, and complained about her standards. He spread rumors that she'd won projects by sleeping with clients and made grievous errors, costing their company revenue and other clients.

Do bullies listen? Will they change? Why should they when they believe they can say "it's my way or the highway" and others will fall into line? Bullies lack internal brakes, rationalize their behavior, and feel justified. While you believe in win/win, bullies hold win/lose beliefs.

Bullies hear what they want to hear: their own rationalizations. When you don't meet a bully's aggression with a firm "halt," he considers you less savvy than he is and, therefore, someone who deserves being walked on. No one deserves that. Hoping for good treatment from a bully is like entering a ring with a bull, believing he'll leave you alone because you're a vegetarian.

Bullies don't need to change—what they do works for them. You give your bully power when you leave it up to him to realize what he is doing and decide to improve. Marie didn't realize this in time and paid for it with her self-esteem. Instead of hoping in vain that a bully will realize that his actions hurt you and change, you are the one who needs to change—both your words and actions—in order to outsmart the bullies in your work life.

Chapters 9 through 20 offer specific strategies for making bullies change their ways.

BULLY TRAP #4:
DIMINISHMENT—REACTING ANGRILY OR STOOPING TO THE BULLY'S LEVEL

SILENT GRENADE MIKE scared nine out of ten employees. "He's spooky," said an employee who quit after a week, "sort of like the psycho Hannibal Lecter in *Silence of the Lambs*."

Big Mitch "fought fire with fire," and paid for it with his job and subsequent damage to his career. When Mike barked at him, Mitch growled back. When Big Mitch continued speaking after Mike interrupted him, a jaw-tightened, white-faced Mike gave Mitch "the stare," telling him to sit up straight during a staff meeting. Although everyone in the meeting temporarily stopped breathing, Big Mitch simply stared back at Mike.

In a fury, Mike ended the meeting, slamming the door as he left the conference room. Mitch followed him. Mike wheeled around, saw him, and jabbed his fingers at Mitch's eyes. Mitch reached out, grabbed Mike's fingers, and twisted them backward. Mike pulled his hand back, and hollered "You're out of here!" "You bet I am!" shouted Mitch.

After Mitch left, everyone breathed easier until the police came. Mike filed assault charges against Mitch, saying Mitch had attacked him without provocation after staring at him like a lunatic. Although Mitch's attorney contacted them, no other employee contested Mike's version of the incident. Mitch lost his job and added an arrest to his résumé.

While few targets fight back as aggressively as Mitch did, some bully victims get angry and seek revenge by "giving back as good as they got." They've finally "had enough" and get nasty.

This rarely works. When you use bullying tactics, you look like the bad guy or at least seem to be as much of a problem as the bully. You may even enable the bully to play the victim to a duped audience.

Further, bullies have years of experience fighting dirty, giving them the advantage if you climb into the ring. As a result, you generally lose. Worse, you wind up regretting how you acted.

Don't fall into this trap by letting a bully push you into being less than the quality professional person you are. Take a deep breath, assess the situation, and act rather than react. Olivia succeeded in this when she encountered a bully on a brutally hot summer day.

SOON AFTER OLIVIA started a new job, her coworkers told her their manager, Jerry, enjoyed bullying and sexually harassing women and quickly fired anyone whose skills threatened him.

"What's he still doing here?" Olivia asked.

"So far it's been the women's word against Jerry's. Besides, Jerry has powerful friends in the industry and management doesn't want to act.

They're a bunch of male chauvinists. They believe the women who speak up are 'uppity, complainers, and neurotic.' Besides, Jerry never does it around anyone, so it's always he said/she said."

When Olivia received an email from Jerry announcing his intention to conduct her thirty-day review at his house, she emailed back, "Not your office?" Jerry replied, "I'm feeling a bit under the weather, but this job review is crucial to your future."

Olivia arrived at Jerry's dressed in a tailored business suit with two copies of the monthly sales report she'd slaved over for hours that morning. She'd worked through lunch; she was starving.

When she knocked on the partially open front door, Jerry called, "Come in, shut the door, and come out back!" She found Jerry drinking a beer on the back deck, dressed in a tank top and a pair of baggy cutoffs. He sprawled on a beach chair. Next to him was an open cooler; on a small table sat a plate of olives. Jerry picked up a giant olive and sucked it suggestively, saying, "I can't get enough . . . of these." Shocked, and already boiling in her suit in the blazing sun, Olivia just stared.

"So, sit, what do you want to tell me, about you-u-u," her manager said. Olivia handed him her report. He tossed it aside. Olivia said, "I'll be glad to talk through my projections."

"Projections?" Jerry asked, ogling Olivia's chest.

When Olivia just stared back at him, Jerry scowled and began telling her everything wrong with her as a salesperson. Although he hired her because she had excellent skills, Jerry really believed that women had no place in sales, which he went on to explain. Olivia reached into her jacket pocket and pressed the record button on her smartphone.

"My sales figures in the report you just tossed away speak to my ability," Olivia stated in a clear, crisp voice.

"Figures," Jerry slurred, leering at Olivia's chest and looking pleased with himself. He patted his lap. "It's hot, why don't you take off your jacket and come sit here, and we'll talk about your fig . . . ures."

"On your lap?" Olivia asked, again in a clear voice.

"Something wrong with your hearing?" Jerry said, patting his lap.

Olivia wheeled around, as Jerry called out "bye-bye." She then went straight to Kinko's and made five copies of her time-dated recording, one each for the company's CEO and Human Resources officer, another for the state's Human Rights Commission, and one for her attorney and herself. Instead of sinking to her boss bully's level, Olivia took prompt, decisive action, and Jerry learned that regulatory agencies didn't like managers who demeaned and sexually harassed employees.

BULLY TRAP #5: SUBMISSION—PLEADING, APOLOGIZING, OR GIVING IN

KARLA SPREAD STORIES about Anne based on nuggets of information she gleaned after plying Anne with wine. When Anne confronted Karla, Karla denied any knowledge of the stories.

Anne knew better and pleaded, "Please stop doing this."

"Can't help you," Karla responded.

"Karla, I'm desperate," Anne begged.

Did begging work? No.

In Chapter 1, Arielle mercilessly took advantage of Tova. After Arielle stiffed Tova twice, Tova said in a soft voice, "The first one's my treat, of course; but do you think you could pay me back for one of them?" When Arielle gave Tova her "are you kidding me?" look, Tova backed off. Later Tova said, "I don't mean to be pushy." "Then don't be," was Arielle's response.

When you beg, plead, or give in, you signal that your bully has the upper hand—not a wise move as bullies believe that weak individuals deserve poor treatment. Stop expecting compassion from bullies. They respect only strength and power.

What makes bullies change? Negative consequences to them.

Climb out of this trap by remembering what matters to your bully: herself and her needs. Show bullies what they win or lose if they treat you differently. Don't be afraid to firmly and professionally dish out negative consequences as Annette (Chapter 1) demonstrated when she forwarded bully Andy's stormy email to their supervisor and Human Resources. For more insights on alternatives to pleading, check out Chapters 9 and 10.

BULLY TRAP #6: PASSIVITY—NOT STANDING UP TO OR APPEASING THE BULLY

Those who work around loud-mouthed, negative, complaining bullies like Chapter 4's Camille often think they chose the right path by listening obediently and remaining passive.

Other targets try to appease their bullies. When you let bullies push you around because they may get "ugly" if you don't, you play a losing game. Bullies know others back down in the face of aggression, so they play your fear to their advantage. Never make an unhealthy compromise to prevent a confrontation. If a bully criticizes you unfairly (and yes, the bully realizes it's unfair) and you back off, you show the bully you can be pushed around.

Further, because Camille-type bullies view those who listen as "on their side," you inspire true fury when you "betray" them by later voicing contrary opinions. Worse, when you try to appease a bully, you erode your own self-esteem to the point where you may feel you deserve the bullying you receive.

Bullies hesitate, however, to joust with those willing to stand up to them. Jillian proved this.

JILLIAN HAD JUST been hired as a contract employee for a large computer networking company and assigned a desk next to Nellie. Nellie and Jillian were given space in the accounting area, on a different floor from their IT coworkers, because their manager wanted Nellie to orient Jillian and there wasn't room for both women in the network administration area. The move angered Nellie.

On her first day, Jillian greeted Nellie by saying, "Hi, I'm looking forward to working with you. I hope we can be good teammates."

"Because of you, I'm stuck over here," Nellie said, glowering. "Hopefully, not for long."

The next week Nellie put in a request to be moved back to the network administration area. When she learned her request had been denied, she threw a temper tantrum.

"I'm sorry," Jillian said. "I can't do anything about it."

"You could leave," snarled Nellie.

The next day, Nellie sent Jillian a lengthy email saying she noticed an odor emanating from Jillian. "It's not a bad odor—you don't stink; it's just that I'm sensitive to something you're wearing." Nellie copied the Human Resources representative who visited both Nellie and Jillian. The HR officer asked Jillian, "Could you avoid any fragrances, including ones in your shampoo, conditioner, laundry detergent, and body lotion?"

"Sure," said Jillian.

Two days later, Nellie emailed Jillian, copying HR, "There's still an odor."

Jillian emailed back, also copying HR. "It isn't me. I wish it was. I could fix it if it was me. I know you want to sit with the others in IT, but I'm surprised; surely there must be odors in that larger group."

"That," said Jillian, "stopped her cold."

Climb out of the "maybe if I appease them, they'll let me be" trap by deciding you'll stand up to the bully. For strategies on how to do this, read Chapters 9 through 11.

BULLY TRAP #7: GULLIBILITY—BELIEVING LIES AND CHASING TRUMPED-UP ISSUES

Bernard, the drill sergeant want-to-be boss (Chapter 4), made up bogus stories accusing his employees of problems they'd supposedly caused coworkers or customers. When Bernard's targets apologized or asked their coworkers or customers what they'd done to offend, they learned the coworkers or customers hadn't accused them of anything. As a result, they felt embarrassed.

Pauline intimidated and manipulated head nurse Molly with daily trumped-up problems. Pauline convinced Molly that she had unwittingly exposed the clinic to serious legal and risk management problems by ignoring arcane regulations. Molly wasted weeks searching for remedies to the problems she had allegedly caused and was so devastated by Pauline's accusations that she avoided talking to the physicians, the one group that could have reined in Pauline.

Though Pauline quickly became known for storming into the clinic and accusing others of not handling matters she'd let slide, making some employees cry, she accused Molly of creating a hostile workplace. According to Pauline, an employee had texted her alleging Molly had yelled. Molly, never a shouter, was horrified, wondering how anyone could have accused her, never realizing Pauline had played her.

Bullies can hide in plain sight if they keep your attention and energy focused on confronting phony, trumped-up issues while they plan or perfect their onslaught. Sidestep this trap. Never take what a bully says at face value. If you're falsely accused, call the bully on it with humor as in "nice try," or by firmly stating "not a chance." You'll find strategies on how to do this in Chapters 9 and 11.

BULLY TRAP #8: ISOLATION—LETTING THE BULLY CUT YOU OFF FROM OTHERS

After Chapter 1's Martin trashed Laura's reputation to her clients and others in the industry, Laura avoided industry gatherings. Before this happened, Laura had regularly called clients to check in with them. Now, Laura stopped calling, fearing they'd heard the mean stories. As a result, some began to wonder if the rumors they'd heard were true.

Sonja longed to make friends with her coworkers, but every time she tried to join the others for lunch in the break room, Alice smirked at her, making Sonja feel unwelcome. As a result, Sonja ate lunch in her cubicle.

Just as a wolf pack steers a caribou calf away from the herd, bullies isolate their targets. If you allow a bully to isolate you, you give your bully greater control over you, even carte blanche to do as he wishes. You become an easier target. Because you're not around others who could help defend you, the bully can spread rumors about you or even convince others you're the problem.

Never give in to a bully's isolation ploy. Jump out of this trap by making friends with coworkers, acquiring allies, establishing an active relationship with your supervisor, and building a strong reputation.

Bullies don't attack those with allies and a wide, deep power base. If a bully attacks you, your allies can rally support for you and lead others to question the bully's motives and honesty. Coworkers and clients who respect and like you can deter and help you survive a bully's attacks. Bullies don't want to go after someone with powerful allies who might turn on them. If your bully, like Alice with Sonja, makes you feel unwelcome joining others, realize that your bully hopes to deepen your slide into the isolation trap.

Next, given the importance of your supervisor's opinion to your career, never let a bully get between you and your supervisor. Establish a reputation for quality work and a solid work ethic. Carefully document your accomplishments and keep your supervisor informed, so no one can claim that you neglected your work or take credit for your efforts.

It takes sustained effort to build a stellar reputation. Act with integrity at all times. Seize opportunities to increase your visibility and to be seen for the quality individual you are. Or, if like Laura, you had good relationships with clients, never allow a bully to get between you and those who can support you.

Your Turn: Where Are You Now?

If any of the things described below never happened to you, imagine they did and answer the questions as if they had.

1. Have you hoped, like Adam, that a workplace bully would "come around" if you were nice enough? What led you to do so? What happened?
2. When a workplace bully abused you, did you tell your supervisor? Or, like Adam, did you remain silent for fear your supervisor would see it as your problem? What led you to have this fear? What do you wish you'd done instead?
3. Have you tried to ignore that you were bullied because you couldn't believe it was happening? How will you keep yourself from doing this again? When did you finally acknowledge what was happening? What inspired you to deal with reality?
4. Have you given a bully an outpost in your head by taking in what he or she said or did as if it was your fault or you deserved it? What led you to do so?
5. Have you, like Anne, beaten yourself up for falling prey to a bully's manipulation? If so, you're attacking the wrong person. If you were your own best friend, would you say "you're to blame," or would you say "you fell victim and now let's get you safe again"?

6. Has a bully flattened your self-esteem? How?
7. If you were Molly's or Sonja's friend, what would you have told them?
8. Have you fallen into the "expecting the bully to change" trap? How did you climb out, if you did? If you haven't, what might you now do?
9. Have you ever pleaded with or given in to a bully? What led you to beg and how did it make you feel? What was the effect on the bully? What do you wish you'd done instead?
10. What do you think standing up for yourself means in your situation? How do you plan to do it? Pick a method and start putting it into practice within twenty-four hours.
11. Has a bully ever led you astray with a trumped-up accusation? What led you to fall for it? What will you do differently next time?
12. Has a bully ever made you feel like you couldn't connect with your coworkers or supervisor? What do you or did you risk by letting yourself be isolated?
13. How do you plan to more actively build relationships with others so you're not isolated or such easy prey? Take two steps this week toward increasing your network or deepening your work relationships.
14. How would you describe your relationship with your supervisor? Take steps this week to increase your communication with your supervisor so you'll have an open channel should you need it.
15. How do you plan to keep your supervisor aware of your efforts, the quality of your work, and your work ethic? What will the positive effect of providing your supervisor regular emails on your accomplishments be? Develop a strategy for documenting your successes. Take at least one step to implement your strategy within the next seven days.

16. What's your visibility within your organization? Are there ways you can strengthen it?
17. What's your reputation? What reputation do you want? What is your game plan for enhancing your reputation? Chapter 22 offers a step-by-step method for creating a game plan for this or any other goal you select.

HOW TO OVERCOME THE BULLY'S FAVORITE WEAPON—AN OUTPOST IN YOUR MIND

I was always looking outside myself for strength and confidence, but it comes from within. It is there all the time.

—ANNA FREUD

ON HER FIRST day of work, Julie's supervisor sat her down and told her Stevie would orient her. Julie waited hours for Stevie to arrive and then sought her out.

Stevie didn't waste any time telling Julie that she wasn't the applicant Stevie would have hired. Hurt, Julie asked, "Why?" Stevie said in a frosty voice, "It's obvious. You've only worked in a small, family-owned business and don't have the sophistication this corporate position needs. You don't even dress properly."

Julie swallowed her pride, pushed her hurt aside, and told Stevie she knew she could learn if Stevie coached her. Stevie twisted her mouth scornfully and turned back to her computer screen. Julie, not knowing what to say, left the room. Julie tried to pretend that what Stevie said didn't get to her, but it did.

Stevie's "orientation" consisted of giving Julie a list of manager and employee names with phone extensions and telling her where she could park her car and find a bathroom. When Julie questioned Stevie about where to find documents on the server, Stevie told her she'd learn her way around the server best if she explored it by herself, and she needed to stop expecting others to do her work for her.

Stevie did, however, act as Julie's personal fashion police, with daily insults about her makeup or what she wore. A typical exchange went like this: "You should go to Nordstrom and get a new pair of shoes."

"What's wrong with these?" Julie asked.

"If you need to ask," Stevie said, in a dill pickle-sour voice, "well, look around at what everyone else is wearing."

Julie looked at her shoes, saw a couple scuff marks, and responded, "I'll wear a different pair tomorrow."

"I doubt those will be any better," scoffed Stevie, turning on her stylish $300 heels and heading down the hallway.

Judgmental bullies like Stevie lurk in many organizations. Give them minor power and they use it to knock others down so they can feel taller. Like mosquitoes that fuel themselves on human blood, they feed off your reaction to their words—the subsequent humiliation, fear, or compliance that results from their intimidation of you. If you redden, wince, look down or away, or say "that hurts," you give these parasites a free ride. These bullies try to control you at a deep level, attacking your own sense of yourself.

THE BULLY WANTS TO TURN YOU AGAINST YOU

Don't allow a judgmental bully's venom to seep into your brain. While you can clearly see vicious Stevie for who and what she is, you may have a harder time seeing how a bully in your work life has played "let's pretend," making you believe her made-up image of you is real. You may even come to believe that there's painful truth to the person's disparaging descriptions of you. That's because a bully's words have the power to hook your attention, enter your mind, and change your outlook on your life, causing you to lose your inner rudder.

To see how quickly this happens, try this experiment: Answer this question out loud—"What color is snow?"

Then, answer this question: "What do cows drink?"

If you responded "white" when asked about snow, you might have said that cows drink "milk" instead of water. How come? The word "white" hooked your attention and entered your mind. Bullies who put you down with their words invalidate you by trespassing across your emotional and mental boundaries.

Images also ensnare your mind, such as the image a bully paints of you when the bully "accidentally" allows you to overhear a vicious comment such as "That stupid, fat cow in accounting" or "Did you see how he stammered and the spittle came out of the corner of his mouth?"

Let's experience the power of an image. Imagine that a friend has invited you over for dessert and asks which ice cream flavors you prefer. You say you love chocolate chunk brownie and toasted coconut almond. Your friend puts a scoop of each into a bowl. "But, I'm on a diet," you say. Your friend responds, "That's the best part; these have been made with low-fat, low-sugar, organic fruit, yet taste like the richest ice cream." You're handed a spoon as your friend adds, "Try some of this melted, dark chocolate on top; it has almost no fat." Can you imagine tasting that dessert? If you can, you've just experienced the power of an image created by another's words.

When you mentally ingest a bully's caustic comments, you allow them to poison your self-esteem and weaken your spirit. Once you eat the bully's garbage, it becomes your garbage and you stop believing in yourself, your abilities, and your right to be treated reasonably.

You may even collude with a bully's put-downs by further tearing yourself down. Soon, you're doing the bully's "beat you up" and "beat you down" work in your own mind. You find yourself saying, "He thinks I'm stupid; I wonder if he's right"; "She said I acted like a fool; everyone's probably laughing at me"; or "What's the matter with me anyway? The boss is right: I never do things right." You've thus handed the remote control for your life over to the bully, who uses it to ravage your self-worth.

BECOME YOUR OWN GATEKEEPER: DON'T LET THE BULLY IN

Now that you know what happens inside your head when a bully invades your mental boundaries, you can decide whether you want to give the bully an outpost in your mind or if you prefer to be the gatekeeper who says, "You're not coming in here; I'm in charge of what I think about me."

When you accept a bully's definition of you, you cast aside your own experience. If you wouldn't let another person stomp on your foot or physically slam you off balance, don't let a bully stomp on your spirit, or bump into and push you over inside *your* head. *Don't let a bully rent space in your head; you are the landlord.*

Take the first step by deciding that no one has the right to turn you against yourself. You'll treat nonsense as what it is—something that makes no sense.

BUILD YOUR MENTAL KEVLAR

Take a look at this list of words. Which ones describe you?

Honest	Funny	Intuitive
Caring	Genuine	Perceptive
Generous	Enthusiastic	Good-hearted
Kind	Fair	Open-minded
Loyal	Natural	Fun-loving
Compassionate	Imaginative	Creative
Responsible	Understanding	Resourceful

How many? Ten? Fifteen? All twenty-one? If even five of them fit you, you possess admirable qualities. Have you let a bully brainwash you into forgetting that?

Next, create a list of five more positive words that describe you.

Take a look at your list. Would you want a friend who has the positive qualities you've listed? Of course you would. By creating and affirming your positive attributes, you honor the person you are, and the next time a bully's words try to hitch a ride in your head, you can say "this car's full."

Add depth to your Kevlar. Take a moment to think of two challenges you handled well or at least survived. What do these experiences tell you about your strength and resilience? If you start to pick on yourself over mistakes you've made, take a look at that. How much bully poison in the form of destructive words and labels have you absorbed? How often do you function as your own worst critic? Each time you do, you magnetize yourself to attract bullies. You'll find more about how to change this ingrained pattern in Chapter 11. For now, remember you have the capacity to learn new self-talk and become your own cheerleader. Refuse to play the bully's disenabling game. If you're reading this book, you've survived and have good instincts. You have an inner rudder you can trust as you develop new skills and strategies.

HEAL YOUR INNER WOUNDS BY REPROGRAMMING YOUR MIND

Most of us have one or more emotional Achilles' heels. Bullies aim for these as if they had radar. They can't, however, open wounds you've healed. Do you have some weak areas, perhaps a self-critical statement that rises to the surface when you're having a bad day?

You can nuke any self-doubting statement using a neurolinguistic (the mind's language) programming strategy called "change your mental tape recorder." Pick a statement or "tape" that weakens you—

for example, "I'll never be brave" or "Other people are smarter than I am."

You can dismantle a tape like this by repeating it seven times in seven different ways, until it loses all or much of the power it holds over you. Imagine that you have a tape recorder in your mind. Turn to the dial marked "tape one" on the left front of the tape recorder. Whatever statement or "tape" you've picked, hear it played or said once loudly in your mind. Hear it again said softly. Hear it again said very slowly; then hear it said very quickly as if recorded at hyper-speed. Now hear it with merry-go-round music playing in the background. Hear it again accompanied by Wagnerian music such as the "Ride of the Valkyries," with cymbals clanging and drums banging. Hear it one final time as if Bugs Bunny or another cartoon character, perhaps one with a deep accent or a slight lisp, might say it. Has it become harder to take this "tape" seriously?

Now, turn the dial on the far left off and turn to the dial marked "new tape," on the right front of the tape recorder. Create and let yourself hear, out loud, an affirmative statement, perhaps "I show courage" or "I am ethical and determined." Hear this statement said again and again in a clear, firm, positive voice.

What's the feeling you get? You can uproot any negative statement that's damaged your heart or spirit using the mental tape recorder strategy. Take a moment to write a list of other positive, affirming statements that describe the true you. You're starting to free yourself of the bully's verbal tyranny and to declare your own war of independence.

TAKE BACK YOUR POWER: CONFRONT MENTAL MANIPULATION

You're now ready to let bullies know their cruel remarks slide off you like water off Teflon. Short statements work well. If your bully asks "Where'd you come up with this crap?" or says "You're too sensitive" or "That was a dumb move," respond by saying, "I'm not playing," "Game over," "Nonsense," or "Nice bait." By speaking up, you take back your power and break the spell the bully tried to cast over you.

Your bully may demand, "What do you mean?" or "What game?" If so, you've taken control; your bully is now reacting to you rather than the other way around. Congratulations. You don't need to take a bully's bait or respond to his harmful, negative questions. Just shake your head. You no longer take what a bully says personally; instead, you simply witness a failed attempt to bully you.

Your Turn: Where Are You Now?

If any of the things described below never happened to you, imagine they did and answer the questions as if they had.

1. What bully words or characterizations of you have recently hooked your attention or crept into your mind? Take any one of them, make it into a statement, and practice neutralizing it by using the mental tape recorder strategy. Did this exercise change your outlook? How might changing your outlook change your life?
2. When you read about Stevie putting Julie down, what did you want to say to Stevie? To Julie? What would you like to say to one of the bullies in your work life? If you were your best friend, what would you say to yourself? (By the way, you can be and are your own best friend.)
3. What do you think of the five positive words you wrote about yourself? Place this list in a private computer file or in a paper file you keep in your work area or at home, and add to it regularly. Once a week, take it out, read it aloud, and let those words sink in. What's the impact of being your own cheerleader? Do more personal cheerleading in the coming weeks, until it comes naturally. What's the effect of this cheerleading? Does it start to come naturally? If not, do more of it.

4. Take some time this week to review challenges you've successfully mastered. Reflecting on them, what is true about your determination, resilience, willpower, and inner strength? Take some time to write in your private journal or simply to think about the strong person you are. If you have a close friend you share insights with, tell this friend what you're learning about yourself.
5. Practice the mental tape recorder exercise at least once a week on a tape you want to nuke. When you reflect on the voice you hear in your head as you repeat "tape one," does it sound like a parent? When you hear "tape two," does it sound like your own voice? You may be carrying voices from the past in your head. Replace them with your own voice and statements.
6. Think of a current difficulty you wish didn't exist. How are you reacting to it? What happens to your breathing and muscle tension when you think about it? What feelings does it arouse? What strategies have you employed thus far to handle it?
7. Practice in your own mind statements like "I'm not playing," "Nonsense," "Nice bait," and "Game over." The next time a workplace bully gives you an opportunity for real-life practice, use them out loud on the bully. How did they work? Take some time to enjoy watching attempts to bully you go down in defeat.
8. What other mental habits or attitudes do you want to get rid of? Pick one and work on it this week.
9. What new initiatives would you like to start?
10. Who in your work life tries to control you? What have you learned that can help you stop them?

COUNTERING BULLY TACTICS AND BULLY SPEAK

The credit belongs to the man who is actually in the arena . . . who strives valiantly . . . who at the best knows in the end the triumph of high achievement, and who at the worst, if he fails, at least fails while daring greatly . . . .

—THEODORE ROOSEVELT

WAYNE, THE SCORCHED-EARTH FIGHTER, loved blaming everything that went wrong on his business partner, Marie. Although he oversaw fiscal management, when taxes came due, he castigated her for not figuring out how to scam the IRS, although doing so was clearly illegal. Although he angered clients, he held Marie accountable for those they lost to other vendors. When revenue dropped, he accused Marie of not marketing more vigilantly.

Bullies wield a variety of tactics and weapons in an effort to dominate and win. They subject you to a stream of verbal abuse, snide comments, insulting emails, and threats; blame you for everything, including their own flaws; publicly humiliate you; hide behind a Dr. Jekyll shield; manipulate you; make unreasonable demands; and exploit you to meet their own needs.

Although these tactics can devastate you, like Dorothy in *The*

Wizard of Oz, you can claim victory by exposing the tactics to light. When Toto jerked the curtain back he showed the wizard for what he was, a shriveled old man working the levers to create an illusion. When Dorothy threw a bucket of water on the Wicked Witch of the West, the witch melted. Let's draw the curtain back to expose workplace bullies, with our water bucket in hand ready to be tossed. You can defeat bully tactics.

VERBAL ABUSE, SNIDE COMMENTS, AND INSULTING EMAILS

Like a dog chewing on a bone, bullies gnaw away at your vulnerabilities, until you crack wide open, humiliated and demeaned. Patricia Evans, author of the classic text *The Verbally Abusive Relationship,* describes verbal abuse as a "kind of battering which doesn't leave physical evidence," but "is often more painful because it lingers in the mind of its target."

Evans says bullies verbally abuse "as a means of holding power over" their targets and to "negate the perceptions, experience, values, and accomplishments of those they target. Bullies constantly invalidate the targets' reality, insidiously blaming, accusing, and confusing them."

Four Ways to Defuse Verbal Abuse

Defeat this bully tactic with four strategies.

Strategy #1: Neutralize Your Bully's Attacks. Build and memorize an arsenal of statements and questions that swiftly neutralize verbal attacks. A flatly uttered "Give it a rest" lets your bully know you're calling "game over." You can ask "What?" or "Pardon me?" as if you can't believe the bully meant the insulting remarks. A calm "Your point?" says you don't think the bully has made one and may even place the bully on the defensive. If the bully persists and asks "Do you have a problem with your hearing?" you can say "No, I wanted to give you a chance to remove your foot from your mouth."

Strategy #2: Refuse to Play by the Bully's Rules. If you don't play along, you witness a failed attempt to bully you. Exit the situation as Annette did when Andy barked at her. In contrast, Suzanne endured Andy's screaming, thinking the situation would get better; she finally quit because she couldn't stand the continued abuse.

Strategy #3: Document What's Happening. Use your digital voice recorder, pocket DVR, or webcam. Connect with witnesses who can provide corroborative evidence to help you confront and defeat the bully.

Strategy #4: Detox Each Night. Bullies wear you down. Worse, you help them by taking their words and actions home with you. At night, you might think about all the things you didn't or couldn't say in your own defense. You might even dream about the bully's continued attacks. As a result, you wake up exhausted and dread returning to work.

As discussed in Chapter 8, don't give the bully an outpost in your mind. Bullies deny your abilities, intentionally devaluing you as a person and an employee. Get their toxic thoughts out of your head and externalize them by writing the bully a letter that says everything that needs to be said. You don't need to mail this letter, just seal it, and give yourself closure. Make each night a vacation from your bully.

THE BLAME/SHAME GAME

Bullies like Wayne delight in berating and ridiculing their targets mercilessly. Because they refuse to take responsibility or feel guilt, they justify what they do by blaming others. These bullies accuse you of their sins, and once they convince you that you're the problem, they feel they're off the hook. Ask bullies why they explode in rage, and they'll say you made them do it because you screwed up, challenged them, or stood in their way.

Bullies excel at projecting their shortcomings onto you. If you're a good person and a bully says, "You're not treating me well," it leads you to question yourself. Thus, bullies twist you into emotional and mental knots and chip away at your confidence. Once they cause you to look anxiously at yourself, they draw your attention to your most negative qualities, lowering your self-esteem and making you more susceptible to their control.

When you acquiesce, you fulfill their need to control. They lash out if you start to slip away. Though he treated her with contempt, Wayne hated Marie for leaving their partnership. He wanted her to remain under his thumb—his personal whipping girl.

Have bullies projected their behavior onto you, accusing you of flaws they refuse to admit in themselves? Have bullies focused on splinters in your eyes rather than the planks in their own? Have bullies convinced you that any problems in your work relationship or situation are your own fault?

The Best Defense Against the Blamer: A Good Offense

A bully's blame/shame attacks can lead you into defending instead of asserting yourself. Douse blame/shame with the cold water of reality. Step back and look at what's really happening. An ancient fable poses this scenario: You show up at your teacher's house for a class. The teacher invites you in and offers you tea. You're thirsty and start to pick up the cup. The teacher pulls out a large stick and says, "If you pick up the cup, I will hit you with this stick. If you don't pick up the cup, I'll hit you." If you were the student, what would you do?

Some sit frozen in indecision, others drink the tea, knowing that the blow will come but preferring that option to being hit and remaining thirsty. An educated target takes the stick from the teacher and says, "I don't like either choice." Others might choose to exit the house, leaving the teacher, tea, and stick behind. Many bully blamers, like the teacher, present you with a no-win situation in which it's "heads you lose, tails you lose." If Marie leaves the partnership, she abandons her investment; if she stays, she endures Wayne's verbal "stick."

Don't let a blamer trap you and then take you apart piece by piece, as Wayne did to Marie. Stand strong, before the blame/shame game depletes your self-esteem and you can neither protect yourself nor think straight. Declare what *you* see as the truth. Having the courage of your convictions requires that you have conviction. Don't let anyone, even you, disrespect you.

THE PUBLIC HUMILIATION GAME

While some bullies attack in private, others prefer to pounce on their targets in front of an audience. Bullies know the pressure watching eyes and listening ears have on some targets. Perhaps you are one of those who immediately wilt from embarrassment. It gave Geoff a special thrill to watch Adam back down in front of other staff members when he challenged Adam's statements during staff meetings. Bullies know when they get under your skin, and, if you let them, they own you.

The Best Defense Against the Humiliator: Never Let It Show

If a bully takes you on in front of an audience, deny her the victory she seeks. Just as a wounded swimmer attracts sharks, if you blush, stammer, or cry, you reward the bully, who uses your embarrassment as an additional weapon. When you don't squirm, you decrease the bully's interest in you as the victim.

Don't let a bully's psychological daggers foot-sweep you into reacting. Desensitize yourself using the coastline breathing and alternate focus strategies outlined in Chapters 5 and 7, respectively. Controlling your breathing also helps you use your adrenal response. Instead of being ruled by it and thrown into choosing between "fight" and "flight" reactions, adrenaline plus breathing links your brain's left and right hemispheres, adding creativity to your thinking and sharpening your wits.

Two can play the crowd game. Turn the situation on the bully with a "Is that the best you've got?" comment. Instead of remaining a doormat walked on by an ambitious employee, Adam could have taken charge of his staff meeting by saying, "Geoff, can't you find a more professional way to handle yourself than to try to 'take me down a peg'?" or "Geoff, you're insulting me in front of your coworkers and my staff. I'd like them to have the chance to make up their own minds about what I'm proposing. I'll be glad to talk with you about your views after the meeting."

Other statements that stop the bully's show include "Does it make you feel good to try to make me feel bad?" and "You're at it again, putting me down so you can feel good about yourself. I don't appreciate it."

In Chapter 1, Tova sought empathy or pity by responding, "That hurts" when Arielle asked, "Do you know your name's a four-letter word?" If Tova had instead said, "That's not even funny," Arielle's audience would have seen Tova standing up for herself.

If you're unsure about what to say, take a deep breath and exit the situation with dignity. Even if you can't speak, you can still walk away. If you leave under your own power, you can consider your retreat an "advance in a new direction."

You may find it easier to confront your bully in private, depriving the bully of the chance to play to an audience. You might say, "I won't let you embarrass me in front of others a second time. Try it again and I'll surprise you."

SHAPE-SHIFTER: DR. JEKYLL TO THE WORLD, MR. HYDE TO YOU

Bullies like Caren use both Mr. Hyde/Dr. Jekyll and passive-aggressive antics to confound their targets. As masters of spin, these bullies confound you by pretending to be innocent. Even though you know deep down that they're bullying you, you may feel you're crazy for suspecting them when others see only their surface charm. When you try to show others what the bully is doing, you may meet a wall of disbelief. Sometimes, you're not even sure you believe yourself. You may even wonder "why me?" as they reserve their Mr. Hyde persona just for you.

Bullies using this tactic exact secret revenge through covert jabbing and sneaky sabotage. When you confront shape-shifter bullies directly, they feign they've been misunderstood and act as if you're being unfair or paranoid.

The Best Defense Against Mr. Hyde: The Truth Will Set You Free

If your bully uses these tactics, don't let it get to you. If you give up or show your exhaustion, it gives the bully a sense of accomplishment, and you lose any leverage you have.

Don't waste your time trying to get these bullies to admit their strategies. You don't need their agreement; if you wait for it, you wait in vain. Instead, counter their tactics by grabbing hold of the truth and calmly, rationally describing the exact behavior you see.

THE PSYCHOLOGICAL MANIPULATION GAME

When Arielle asked Tova to bring her a latte, she played on Tova's natural expectation that no one would ask someone else to purchase something for her without intending to reciprocate. When bully Pauline discovered how much nurse Molly cared about doing a good job and caretaking their clinic, she alleged Molly's ignorance had exposed the clinic to potentially devastating risk, knowing the psychological damage this twist of the knife would wreak on Molly.

Bullies like Arielle and Pauline manipulate overtly or covertly in an attempt to control your actions and thoughts. Controlling you is the barometer by which bullies validate their identity. They attack and push until you focus your energy on defending yourself and can no longer assert who you are and so give in to what they want. They lash out at you for what you haven't done *and* for what you have done.

The Best Defense Against the Manipulator: Exposure

Pull the Wizard of Oz's curtain back and expose these psychological maneuvers. What motive or intention do your bully's actions and statements have? Do they wise you up for your sake or tear you down contemptuously? Don't let bullies hide in plain sight by manipulating you; instead, keep your eye on them.

Keep your wits about you and step outside their manipulative games. If your habit is to kowtow or lash back, *never* use the first words that come to mind or you may say something you'll live to regret. Tova could have defeated Arielle's con job by saying, "I learned yesterday that lattes cost $5 here. Do you have cash or will you write me a check for what you'd like me to get you today?"

Finally, watch your back with your own personal Karla, knowing bullies happily use whatever you divulge against you. When you work with bullies who manipulate, don't give them ammunition. Anne made this mistake when Karla plied her with wine and false camaraderie, which led her to reveal damaging personal information. Anything you say to a bully can and may be used against you.

THE EXPLOITATION GAME

Boss, employee, and coworker bullies often make unreasonable demands, leading their targets to feel that they're the bad guy if they say "No." A bully boss may pile an extreme workload on you, refuse your leave requests, and look askance when you attempt to leave work at a reasonable hour. A bully employee may ask for more and more time off or other favors or perks, leading you to take on his or her duties when you can't shift them to the bully's coworkers. A bully coworker may ask you for a "just this one time" favor every day.

Bullies run rampant over you and others without worrying about the consequences to you; they simply don't care.

The Best Defense Against the Exploiter: Just Say "No"

If you're asked for the unreasonable and instinctively give in because you like to please, take a moment to consider "What exactly has this bully asked for?" and "Would I ask anyone for the same thing?" If you answer "No," you have your answer. Don't allow your kindness to lead you into exploitation.

THE INTIMIDATION GAME

In Chapter 4, bully boss Bernard threatened his entire staff with job loss by declaring they deserved to be fired and proclaiming, "There is blood in the water." Other bullies menace and terrorize by demonstrating their explosive tempers or by telling you what they plan to do to you if you don't fall in line. Bullies threaten because threats work. They know that all they need to do to make you give up is to get ugly.

The Best Defense Against the Intimidator: Take a Time-Out

If you're threatened verbally, give yourself time to clear-headedly assess what's in your best interests. You can stop the action with a statement such as "I'd like to have some time to think about it." This short-circuits the bully's plans and helps you avoid being pushed into acquiescence with mental strong-arm tactics.

Although you need to take any threat seriously, most bullies test to see what you're made of and behave as badly as you'll allow them to. If it won't endanger you, summon the courage to speak up and remind the bully that his actions have consequences. Sometimes a simple "You're not getting away with that here" reminds the bully that you'll hold him accountable for his actions. Bullies hate to suffer, and if you can reverse the risk/benefit ratio they seek, they may look elsewhere for easier prey.

Warning: If you fear physical violence and your employer won't or can't protect you, or happens to be the culprit, contact the police. They take bullying that crosses the line into threatened or real physical assault seriously.

Whether the threat is verbal or physical, you'll want to keep records so you can present a detailed account of unfair behaviors. If possible, you may want to audiotape any threat to allow you to enlist assistance from a senior manager, your Human Resources officer, a regulatory agency, or the police.

Your Turn: Where Are You Now?

If you have not encountered any of these situations, imagine what it would be like if you had, and answer the following questions accordingly.

1. Has a bully hammered away at your vulnerabilities? How did you handle it? How will you now handle bully speak?
2. Have you ever mentally taken a bully home with you? How will you detox next time?
3. Has a bully shamed you? What happened? What will you do next time?
4. Has a bully publicly humiliated you? What happened? What words or strategies will you use next time?
5. Has a passive-aggressive or Dr. Jekyll/Mr. Hyde bully tied you in knots? How did you handle it? How will you counter these tactics next time?
6. Has a bully manipulated you? If you faced this same manipulation today, what could you do instead?
7. Has a bully made unreasonable demands or exploited you? How? In what ways can you handle it?

8. Has a bully threatened you? What was said or done? How did you extricate yourself? What do you wish you'd done instead?
9. Choose the tactic you find hardest to deal with. Imagine the bully employing this tactic on you. Enact the entire scenario in your mind in the way you'd like to handle it.

10

TURN THE TABLES ON A BULLY WITH ONE EASY MOVE

You gain strength, courage, and confidence by every experience in which you really stop to look fear in the face. . . . You must do the thing you think you cannot do.

—ELEANOR ROOSEVELT

"YOU SURE SCREWED UP," Wayne snarled.

Marie's stomach plummeted, as all eyes turned to her. She braced herself for what was coming. Wayne had given her an impossible assignment, to make a penny-pinching client, who wanted Mercedes results without paying for them, happy. She'd worked days, nights, and weekends, but in the end the client had taken the templates Marie created and refused to pay, saying he'd expected more.

What could she say? If she said no one could have succeeded on the project, she'd sound defensive. If she argued that she'd done the best she could, Wayne would simply heap more abuse on her. Better to keep her mouth shut.

GAIN CONTROL: ASK A QUESTION

Bullies excel at preemptive attacks that leave you defensive, flustered, and tongue-tied. They slice open their targets with nasty statements. Do you want to turn the tables on the bully in your work life? Here's how.

If I yell at you and you yell back, who has the upper hand? I do. I created a confrontation and you reacted. Even, and especially, if you retaliate in fury, I still win because I pushed your button and you reacted.

If I yell at you and you get defensive, who has the stronger position? Again, I do. I set the game in motion and you played it.

What happens if I yell at you and you respond with a question? Although it may seem like I'm still in charge, you've just taken control of the encounter. Here's an example. If I yell at you, "Is that all you got done?" and you respond, "I'm sorry; it took longer than I'd planned," I've placed you on the defensive. If you attack me by saying angrily, "You have no clue," you're still playing my game. If, however, you ask "What would you like me to work on next?" you take over the lead position, forcing me to answer your question.

Imagine that a bully attacks you accusingly, "Where'd you come up with this crap?" Regardless of how you answer, you'll probably sound defensive, making it open season for the bully to continue. If instead you counter with "What are you getting at?" you turn the tables.

Here's another example. Your bully yells, "You're an irritating fool!" You lose if you yell back, "It's you who's irritating." You've simply shown the bully that he can push your button. What if you insist "I'm not irritating"? Yeah, right. Now you sound defensive. If instead you ask, "What was irritating?" you turn the tables and force the bully to respond to you.

What if the bully knows you're sensitive about your appearance and says to you, "You look like a dog"? You might redden and tighten your jaw in response to this snarky comment. If others are watching, they may pity you. But what if you responded, "What breed?" The table is turned.

When you ask a question, you sidestep an attack and take control of the conversation. If your bully confronted you in front of an audience, they then laugh with and not at you.

Suppose your bully slams you as you're giving him instructions by saying, "You're confusing me." If you ask, "Where'd I lose you?" you make his statement a problem to be solved, and avoid the bully's blaming message. If your bully insults a presentation you're making by saying, "You're boring me," and you ask, "What would make this more interesting?" you assume the stronger position.

Questions also help you avoid the "yes/no" trap. If your bully asks, "Do you cut your own hair?" with a tone that implies you have a lousy haircut, whatever you answer, you lose. If you instead ask, "And why is this important to you?" you take the upper hand.

Occasionally, bullies smirk and say "Just kidding" after they've jabbed you. If you protest, they push you further, by asking, "Why are you making a big deal about this?" thus blaming you for feeling stung. Again, a question works best.

Contrast:
THE BULLY: "You're a fool."
YOU: "What!"
THE BULLY: "Just kidding."
YOU: "I don't think so."
THE BULLY: "Look, don't make such a big deal out of this."

With:
THE BULLY: "You're a fool."
YOU: "Really?"
THE BULLY: "Just kidding."
YOU: "Really?"

Questions work even better than an apology.

Contrast:
THE BULLY: "You didn't listen to me."
YOU: "I'm sorry."

With:
THE BULLY: "You didn't listen to me."
YOU: "What did I miss?"

After you've turned the tables on the bully with a question, slam the door shut on the conversation with a flat statement that takes the wind out of your bully's sails. For example:

THE BULLY: "You didn't listen to me."
YOU: "I've heard enough."

Or, make a statement in the form of a question:

YOU: "Is that the best you can do?"

Another phrase that works is, "You just did it again," which forces your bully to ask, "What do you mean?" allowing you to say, "Attack me." If the bully then says, "You're too sensitive," you can ask, "Compared to whom?" taking the lead back.

When you ask a question, you are saying, "I'm strong enough to hear another's opinion. I don't wilt under the bully's scorn, or cower when the bully blasts me. I don't pretend to be perfect." To the bully, you state confidently, "Lay it on me. Take your best shot. Game on." Notice what happens internally when you do this. Questions protect you in a way that neither retaliating nor defending yourself does.

When you fight in response to an attack, particularly if your face has turned red and your mouth tightened, you signal to yourself, the bully, and anyone watching that the bully has pushed you into a reactive mode of fight, flight, or freeze.

Similarly, defensiveness accomplishes little and demonstrates you've let the bully get to you. Even as you're outwardly defending yourself, you may quail inwardly. Worse, after the encounter, you may wonder if the bully's right, that you're somehow less of a person than he.

So turn the tables. Train yourself to ask a question when attacked.

Your Turn: Where Are You Now?

1. When you're attacked, what happens inside you? Do you get angry? Defensive? Are you intimidated?
2. What happens mentally and physically to you? Do you stop thinking? Breathe faster? Feel your heart pound?
3. When a bully judges you, do you start to judge yourself?
4. Practice responding to the following attacks with questions:
   - Where did you come up with this crap?
   - You are impossibly dumb.
   - You're a bitch.
   - Can't you ever do anything right?
   - How could you be so stupid?
   - You moron.
   - You really made a mess of that.
   - You're a fat cow.
5. For the next three days, ask a question whenever a bully makes a statement, asks a question, or looks at you in a way that attacks or puts you down.

11

CREATE THE YOU WHO WON'T KNUCKLE UNDER

The world breaks everyone and afterward many are strong at the broken places.

—ERNEST HEMINGWAY

ANNE THOUGHT SHE'D put the Karla nightmare behind her when she started her new job. She'd taken a work break, gotten her master's degree, and moved from Chicago to Portland. But she hadn't counted on Eudora.

"I was reading about you," Eudora smiled, sidling up to Anne in the break room.

"Reading?"

"Pretending not to know?"

Anne felt a sudden sick feeling in her stomach.

"I love to research new hires, especially those who move from out of state. Fascinating Facebook posts about you; the men in our company have so much to look forward to."

The nausea in Anne's stomach turned to ice. Would she have to leave this job too?

What does it take to stop bullies?

You—and your ability to outsmart them.

Bullying produces results for the bully. If you don't want to be steamrolled or trampled, you have to become someone who can and will stand up to and outmaneuver bullies. This means you need to think and act differently from how you have in the past. The problems you face can't be solved with the same thinking that led you into those problems.

DIG DEEP AND FIND YOUR INNER STRENGTH

How do you grow stronger and become smart and tough enough to take on the bullies in your work life? You start from where you are and grow the skills you need.

Starting from where you are means not judging yourself. For example, let's say you're easily intimidated, and, although you've learned effective strategies from Chapters 3, 6, and 7, you still back down when a bully threatens you. This then is your starting point.

Never worry about not being brave or strong enough. Instead, dig deep inside yourself, into the place from which you draw inner strength. You may have tapped this before. If not, it's where your sense of resolve and willingness to take on a challenge comes from.

A Simple Way to Stop Being a Pushover

If you've never found this place inside yourself before, here's a simple strategy for finding it the first time or for visiting it now. To feel your core strength, create an inner focus. Allow yourself to "feel" the words *centered*, *grounded*, *inner strength*, and *rock solid*. Focus on each word one-at-a-time, not moving on until you *feel* that word. You'll notice that you connect with one or more of those words at a deep level. Close your eyes, and allow yourself to completely experience the word or words that resonate most strongly.

In the training sessions I conduct, I have attendees try this in pairs. One person watches her partner doing this inner work and when she sees a look of determination or resolve coming over her partner's face, she puts an arm behind the partner and pushes with her hand against the partner's chest. Participants are always stunned that they can't push over a person who's inwardly focused on words such as *inner strength* or *rock solid.*

One frail woman, who announced ahead of the activity that she wouldn't be able to master it, stood like concrete when her partner pushed against her. "I never would have thought I had that in me," she said. "I imagined I was a massive oak tree with roots going deep into the earth." A week later she sent me a photo she'd taken of a tree she'd drawn, which now hung over her desk.

If you're doing this exercise alone with no one to push you, you may nonetheless notice that a sensation remains with you when you finish the exercise. You may feel stronger and more centered. This is the result of digging deep and reaching the place inside yourself where you find resolve.

You can add to this feeling of strength by reflecting on any mind-opening revelations you've gained from reading the first ten chapters. Insights inspire growth. By verbalizing them, you cement what you've learned in your memory. Give yourself a moment to rejoice in what you have discovered about yourself and the changes you intend to create in your work life and how you relate to your bully.

STEP INTO YOUR POWER

In John 8:32, it says, "Then you will know the truth, and the truth will set you free."

The truth is that you deserve better.

Set yourself free. When a bully confronts you, consider how a brave person would handle the bully or situation, and become that brave person. Unless it compromises your physical safety, be willing to exit your comfort zone. Bullies push and push and push until someone stops them. Find the courage to express what you want.

Voice your views clearly so your bully can't miss hearing what you've said. "I" statements work when both parties are operating from a win/win mindset; "you" statements have the directness bullies can't ignore. "Do not insult me" proves stronger than "That upsets me" and defines a firm boundary for what you will and won't allow. Even if speaking honestly doesn't change your bully, it bolsters you to hear yourself saying what needs to be said.

When you step forward, you're not fragile, passive, or powerless. You're not just letting events happen to you and silently allowing bullies to walk all over you. You're standing up for yourself, knowing you have inner strength.

EMPOWER YOURSELF BY MANAGING MENTAL BARRIERS

The unfairness of being targeted by a bully can tie you in mental knots. Your mind travels each turn of the rope, looking for the elusive end where you hope to find fairness. Even if you untie the knots, you won't find the treatment you deserve. Move past this "it isn't fair" sticking point by developing a game plan that defeats further bullying; that's what will create future fairness.

Turn off Your Blame Button

Bullies excel at projecting their weaknesses onto targets, and adding a dose of shame. Don't allow your blame button to be pushed. Criticize the bully, not yourself. If you buy into the bullies' projections, you relieve them of their accountability and take on their shame burden. Have you been turning yourself inside out to please a bully who will never be appeased? Learn to doubt the bully, not yourself.

Waste no time in finger-pointing. Blame gives away your power by placing the responsibility to change on your bully. To deal with bullying, you need a powerful, solution-oriented focus on what you need to do to stop the bully. Even though the bully's behavior is not your fault, when you take on bullying as your problem, you move toward fixing it.

Don't blame yourself for being bullied and *never* take bullying personally. You didn't create the bully, nor ask to be bullied. The bully's actions project his or her reality, not yours. If you've been trampled in the past, don't berate yourself. Instead, remind yourself of your strengths. For example, do you instinctively give others compassion and warmth? Would you value a warm, compassionate friend? If so, value yourself.

Fight Your Fear

Fear may swamp your fighting spirit. Escape this swamp by owning your fear. Unaddressed fear paralyzes the spirit; however, once you claim your fear, you can use it to sharpen your senses. Fear-generated adrenaline can motivate you to action.

By managing these mental barriers, you empower yourself. When you find the courage to express what you really want, you renew your spirit. When you set goals, make decisions, and follow through on personal commitments for how you'll handle bullying tactics, you overcome former limitations and discover untapped abilities. Taking action strengthens your will.

UPROOT OLD HABITS WITH NEW ACTIONS

Old habits die hard. At first, when you begin handling bullies differently, you may find yourself instinctively reacting with doormat compliance or other unwanted behavior. You can fix this with the "stop, freeze, do anything else but" strategy. This technique helps you catch yourself just as you're about to repeat the past and allows you to create a new future.

The "Stop, Freeze, Do Anything Else But" Strategy

Here's how it works: The moment you notice you're about to react in a way that plays into the bully's hand, stop yourself, and take a different action than the first one that comes to mind. This "anything else but" strategy seems simple, and is. It halts and uproots former habits. For example, imagine a bully insults you and you start to apologize. Stop, mid-sentence if you have to, and say, "Wait, it's you who needs to apologize" or simply look at the bully in disgusted disbelief.

Never punish yourself for a slip backwards into old behaviors. That turns a misstep into a derailment. Instead, stop, freeze, and do something other than your old habit. By doing this consistently, you can discover a new way forward and become an individual who won't knuckle under anymore.

Visualize and Rehearse New Habits

Strengthen your new habits by repeated mental rehearsals. Imagine yourself walking forward with purposeful strides. See yourself making clear, direct statements. Picture yourself doing the right things over and over, duplicating the real-life situation as closely as possible. Picture also what you don't want to happen, and plan how to respond to any worst-nightmare scenarios with poise. Don't imagine yourself intimidated; instead, envision yourself keeping your cool, no matter what. By mentally creating the scene with as many details as possible, and putting yourself into it, you give yourself a safe environment in which to try out your strategies. Visualize yourself doing the right thing from beginning to end, so that you can feel you've been there, and successfully done what you would like to do.

Your Turn: Where Are You Now?

1. What was your first thought when you read the chapter title? Was it excitement or fear? What happened to your confidence level as you read the chapter?
2. Consider your past responses to bullies—perhaps fear, knuckling under, or embarrassment. What places within yourself can you identify that might need strengthening for you to respond to rather than react to a bully's outburst?
3. What thoughts did you have in response to the "dig deep" discussion about not judging yourself? How does it free you to simply consider where you are, with your strengths and fears, or other challenges, as your starting point?
4. Try the dig deep "pushover" exercise with another person. Notice how much more intense the lesson is when you pass it on. Try saying the words *rock solid, steadfast, inner strength,* and *centered*—this time with your eyes open. If one or more of these words gives you strength, write it on several sticky notes. Place one in your work area and one on your bathroom mirror, where you'll see them daily. If you don't want others reading your reminders, simply write the initial letters as in *rs, s, is,* or *c.* Let *is* be an inside joke.
5. What area of your comfort zone or what mental habit or attitude do you want to move past? Select one and work on it this week.
6. Dream a little and think of a new initiative you would like to start; it can even be something that has nothing to do with bullying. When you set goals, you inspire yourself. When you take concrete steps toward your goals, you build your self-confidence.
7. Create a list of four "you" statements that fit situations you have recently encountered. Then say each of them out loud. What happens inside you when you state them? Try saying each of them three times in a row; make your

voice firm and strong. Allow this to be the voice that speaks in your ear.

8. Uproot your habit of criticizing and second-guessing yourself. Here's an experiment: Go cold turkey on self-criticism for the next forty-eight hours. If you catch yourself criticizing yourself, stop, and think of three qualities about yourself you admire, or two things you've done right in the last week.
9. Have you found yourself going in circles with the "it's not fair" mental knot? How would it benefit you if you decided, "I'm the one who can make this situation fair"?
10. In the next two weeks, develop your ability to respond quickly, easily, and effectively to bully jabs. If a bully makes a statement for which you have no response, use the all-purpose "Pardon me?" or a wryly spoken, "Classy . . . *not.*"

    Keep a list of any put-downs for which you lacked a response, and let your creative brain consider them until you create two responses for handling each bully slam. If you find yourself struggling to come up with a response, you can write to me at my website, www.workplacecoachblog.com, and I'll come up with several for you.
11. Try the "stop, freeze, do anything else but" strategy at least once in the next two weeks. You'll find it works to interrupt any pattern you want to discard.
12. Select one scenario you want to practice handling differently, and map out what you'll say and how you'll act. Stick a piece of paper with your bully's name on the wall; stand up and walk through the entire scene, letting yourself imagine the bully's actions and hear the bully's words; counter them with what you want to say on your behalf. Keep your breathing deep and level; keep your head up and back straight.

    How does it feel to stand up for yourself?
    What have you learned from doing this?

You now have a strategy for replaying any scene, including a real one that you don't feel you handled well. Remember, how you handled it was your starting point, and the incident gives you new material on which to practice. From now on, consider each bully in your work life as an unpaid coach, giving you opportunities to perfect your skills.

HOW TO SILENCE THE ANGRY, AGGRESSIVE JERK

Keep away from angry, short-tempered men, lest you learn to be like them and endanger your soul.

—PROVERBS 22:24–25

"VERN, YOU DON'T MIND my busting your balls, do you?" asked Max, a broad-shouldered Marine drill sergeant lookalike with a crew cut, who ran the facilities department for a large oil company. Max's voice sounded like ripping duct tape; he walked with military precision, and shook hands with an anaconda-strong grip.

Most of Max's peers avoided him, and that was the way he liked it, bragging to his staff that others "give him a wide berth." Max hired bullies, and they enjoyed laughing while watching how Max handled the "wusses" in the accounting, client services, and administrative departments.

Once Vern accepted a promotion to head the accounting department, he realized he couldn't avoid Max, as their two departments intertwined. Vern had hated watching Max make the previous accounting department manager his whipping boy.

When Vern engaged me as his coach, I warned him that his practice of biting his tongue when attacked and his win/win approach could prove his undoing with a win/lose operator like Max.

Not always right but never in doubt, the angry, aggressive jerk gets right in your face and tells you off when he's having a bad day or doesn't get what he wants. These arrogant know-it-alls mask incompetence with bombast, pretending everyone else is stupid. Wielding insults as weapons, jerks find and play on your weaknesses and erode the self-esteem of those around them. Jerks like to keep their targets close and under control, as their victims fulfill these bullies' desire for power.

What You Can Expect If You Work with or for a Jerk

- Jerks dominate you, or try to—controlling your time, ear, and physical space—forcing you to adopt a passive role or challenge them.
- Jerks blame, demean, belittle, and insult you.
- If they're your boss, jerks unfairly deny you earned privileges, such as comp time, and stubbornly refuse to recognize your contributions, chipping away at your confidence and potential.

REAL-WORLD TACTICS THAT WORK

You can't ignore a jerk's taunts. These bullies interpret silence as concession and behave as badly as you let them.

When they taunt or berate you, take a deep breath and employ the alternative focus strategy presented in Chapter 6. By centering yourself and appearing calm, you take away some of their fun. Remember, sharks go after a wounded swimmer.

Many jerks shut their ears when their mouths open. As a result, you can short-circuit their verbal violence if you don't take their bait. The turning-the-table and countering strategies in Chapters 8, 9, and 10 work.

If you find yourself pushed by mental strong-arm tactics, stop the action with "You're not getting away with that here" or "I'd like some time to think about what you're saying." If you're being asked to do something objectionable, give yourself time to assess what's being asked, and plan what you'll say.

Tactic #1: Reverse the Risk/Reward Ratio

Bullies don't like to suffer. Reverse the risk/reward ratio they expect when they take you on.

VERN DECIDED TO change Max's perception of how easy it was to trash him and his department. Max's "You don't mind my busting your balls" comment played right into Vern's hands. Realizing Max planned that as his exit line, Vern countered, "Bust my balls? Not a chance. They're tougher than you think. You have no clue."

Unaccustomed to anyone standing up to him, Max was temporarily speechless, though his face reddened and his nostrils flared, as Vern and his assistant left. "Wow, that was amazing; there's a new sheriff in town," Vern's assistant said, but Vern wisely stated, "That was only round one. He'll be back for me."

The next day, Max stormed angrily into Vern's office with copies of several crumpled emails, which he threw on Vern's desk. "What the hell is this crap?" Knowing Max expected him to pick up and smooth out the emails, Vern instead calmly eyed Max. "You're easy."

"What the f--- do you mean, short boy?" Max shouted, towering over Vern, still seated at his desk.

"All I have to do is say something and you react. I can make you angry. That means I own you."

Momentarily at a loss for words, Max almost choked on his spittle; then he reared up and hollered, "You own nothing."

"See, I did it again," Vern stated calmly. "I say something and you get louder."

"Your emails are garbage," Max choked out.

"They outline the rules you need to follow if you want your projects to move forward," Vern said calmly, sweeping the crumpled pages off his desk and into the trash, before standing up. "Now, if you'll excuse me, I have a meeting with our boss."

Not everyone has Vern's guts, however. He reported that Max treated him, and his emails, with more respect after those two encounters.

TACTIC #2: TAKE AWAY THE BULLY'S POWER OVER YOU

Many work with a jerk like Camille. Camille loved forcing others to listen to her diatribes as she slammed her supervisor and coworkers from her "bully pulpit," secure in the knowledge that few listeners felt brave enough to say they disagreed with her assessments or even "I've heard enough. Stop already."

I was hired to provide an "anti-gossip" session by Camille's organization. When I surveyed those who'd be attending, I learned the true problem involved more than gossip. Although gossip existed—employees named Camille as the number one gossiper—the staff felt helpless to stop her once she started her violent monologues bashing someone. Several employees said that no one, not even the organization's manager, wanted to confront Camille. I shared my insights with the manager, who confirmed them.

Like many bullies, Camille refused to participate in training that might empower her targets. She called in sick the morning of the training. The manager called me and asked, "Should we reschedule since Camille won't be there?"

"Don't give her that much power," I answered. During the session, we practiced effective methods for shutting down gossip. For example, if a would-be gossip says, "Do you know what I just heard about Carole?" I suggested responding, "I don't want to hear it" or "I'd rather Carole tell me if it's about her."

If a would-be gossip opens with, "Marcia just said an awful thing about you," I recommended answering, "Let's you and I go find Marcia and have a three-way discussion."

Then, we tackled Camille, without using her name. I explained that those who speak negatively upset us and create an effect that continues long after they finish. Negativity can impact us for hours, unless we create an antidote. The simplest? Write the negative person's name or message in the center of a piece of paper. Then, draw a circle around the name or message and a diagonal line through the circle, similar to a "no smoking" poster.

Look at what you've drawn; notice that you've fenced in the name or message and created the universal "no [fill in the blank]" symbol. Then, scrunch the paper up and toss it in the nearest trash. Two days later, I visited the organization's manager and asked, "How are things going?" She started to laugh and explained that Camille had come to her upset because so many of her coworkers were acting "idiotically."

"I asked Camille what she meant," the manager said, and she said they were ripping up pieces of paper, tossing them in the trash, and laughing.

"It's odd," said the manager, "but you gave us back our sense of humor and with that came power. Camille felt it."

Tactic #3: Fight Fire with Fire

Remember the angry, aggressive jerk Bernard? He paced in front of his staff calling them "inadequate and worthless" and threatened, "Your jobs are in jeopardy." Sam turned in his resignation that day. One of Bernard's employees, Mavis, took a different tack.

A SHORT, FIERY REDHEAD, Mavis proposed to two of her coworkers that they use their iPads and smartphones to tape Bernard's finger-pointing rants. Initially, Mavis and the others saw it as a way to keep their spirits up. One evening, however, Mavis said excitedly, "These are great; we could make a YouTube video and send it to Anderson Cooper for his 'The RidicuList.'

"Count me out," said one coworker, and the others agreed. Mavis wasn't deterred, as she'd found a new job. While she didn't use anything the others gave her, she created the video and asked Bernard for a meeting.

"Do you watch Anderson Cooper?" Mavis asked.

Puzzled, Bernard responded, "Yes, but what's that got to do with your job?"

"I've accepted another job. Here is my letter of resignation; I'm giving you two weeks' notice."

"You're out today!"

"Well, then, please accept my parting gift. It has to do with Anderson Cooper," Mavis said, handing Bernard a DVD.

"What the hell's this?"

"A video starring you," Mavis said with a bright smile, and left.

Bernard couldn't resist. He took the DVD home, put it in his player, and pressed "Play." He saw his face staring back at him; his face reddened and his mouth opened in shock. He heard Mavis saying, "Bernard, if I hear you're continuing your bully storms, I will send this video to Anderson Cooper to air on 'The RidicuList.' I predict, if it airs, it will go viral."

"Before you ask, no one helped me make this. This is just between you and me. But I plan to check back regularly with those I'm leaving in your employ, and if you don't clean up your act, this video will no longer be between you and me; it will be between you and millions of viewers."

Your Turn: Where Are You Now?

If you have not encountered an angry, aggressive jerk, imagine what it would be like if you had, and answer the following questions accordingly.

1. Do you work with a jerk? Which of the three examples does your bully most resemble: Max, Camille, or Bernard? What does your bully do?
2. How does this bully's behavior impact you? How does his behavior impact others?
3. How have you responded to this bully or other angry, aggressive bullies in the past?
4. What tactics (Chapter 9) did your bully use? What traps (Chapter 7) did you fall into?
5. Jerks have several Achilles' heels. They don't like to feel pain; therefore, if you set up a risk/reward ratio not in their favor, they often back down. They believe their own inflated press releases in which they're all powerful; thus, when you stand up to them, they don't know how to take it. They expect you to get upset when they yank your chain, and don't know how to respond when you don't take their bait. How can you use any of these Achilles' heels to change what happens between you and a current or future angry, aggressive bully?
6. Do you work with a bully who aggressively bends your ear with his or her negativity? What do you plan to do the next time this bully talks on and on?
7. What do you admire about the actions Vern took?
8. What do you believe led Max to back down?
9. How do jerks affect morale and productivity?
10. How do others cope with this type of bully? What seems to work? What doesn't work?
11. What advice would you give to someone facing a jerk?
12. Vern used breathing and alternate focus to steady himself. This is a good time to refresh your memory, so try each of them at least once during the next two days.

13

HOW TO HANDLE A SCORCHED-EARTH FIGHTER

Courage is never to let your actions be influenced by your fears.

—ARTHUR KOESTLER

MAURA HAD DONE the right thing. She had fired Elliott, an employee who'd lied on his employment application and expense account, and then created havoc in her small company, holding closed-door meetings with the goal of turning one employee against another. A soft-hearted woman, Maura hated firing anyone and told Elliott she wished him well.

Months later, when she learned Elliott had pirated written materials she'd spent decades developing, she initially sent him multiple letters reminding him the materials weren't his. When her clients began telling her Elliott was still passing her materials off as his, insisting he'd created them and she'd stolen them, she sought legal advice. Her attorney, Ted, told her she had two options. Accept the situation or sue.

"I hate both options," said Maura, "but I can't let this happen; I have too much at stake." She asked her attorney to draft a letter asking her ex-employee to stop using her materials and giving a deadline for their return. When the deadline passed, Ted filed suit.

Predictably, Elliott hired Stuart, the meanest scorched-earth litigator he could find. A short, powerfully built man with a jutting jaw and an incongruous pug nose, Stuart loved legal warfare. He immediately filed a motion asking for Maura's personal and business tax records for the last fifteen years.

"For what purpose?" Maura asked Ted.

"To scare you."

"Should I give them up?"

"No. He thinks he can walk all over you, find things you don't want found, and use that as ammunition to force you to settle."

"Why would I settle? I'm the one who has been wronged."

"Exactly."

Scorched-earth fighter bullies (scorchers) play a "heads I win, tails I win" game. Believing might equals right and lacking a conscience, they attempt to take what they want from the target, and, when they do, they act to destroy the target's reputation.

If you tangle with a scorcher, don't expect fairness or mercy. They threaten until you give in, then they walk all over you, telling themselves, "Anyone who lets me walk on her deserves to be hurt."

AS MONTHS PASSED, Maura felt she was living in the eye of a legal storm. Whenever she received legal paperwork, she heard in her head the humming sound one hears before a tornado.

When Maura met Stuart for the first time, she quailed. He reeked of outrage and self-righteousness. Astonished, she asked Ted, "What's his deal? Surely he knows his client stole from me."

"He doesn't care."

"How could he not?"

"He only wants to win. Right doesn't matter. In fact, it makes it a better win for him because if he prevails he does so despite the odds."

Several times Maura asked Ted if she should call off the suit: "It's taking time and energy away from my business." What Maura didn't say was that she'd been raised in a household in which her older brother had bullied her from toddlerhood, and that fighting—even standing up for herself—devastated her. As a girl, she'd never felt safe from her brother, who seemed to want her gone. She'd learned to hide from him, knowing that she was defenseless because her parents were in denial about the situation.

REAL-WORLD TACTICS THAT WORK

If you face off against a scorcher, avoid providing him or her an excuse to turn on you.

Tactic #1: Stay Under the Radar

In the short term, you may want to stay under the scorchers' radar by giving them the allegiance they desire. As long as you can do so ethically, help them achieve their goals; in that way you won't unleash their rage.

Tactic #2: Protect Yourself; Document Everything

If a scorcher attacks you, don't take it personally. Instead, protect yourself by quickly leaving and documenting the behavior. Store your documentation off-site. Ultimately, your documentation may prove the scorcher's undoing.

Tactic #3: Enlist the Help of Allies

If you are in a protected category because of your age, sex, race, religion, etc., and the scorched-earth bully crosses the line into actions that harass you, seek legal counsel or the help of a state or federal regulatory agency.

It generally takes an outside power to take out a scorcher. If you work in a larger organization, or one governed by a board of directors, seek allies and mentors at a senior management level who can help you. Show them what's happening and what the scorcher costs the organization to induce them to act. You'll find guidance on how to make a case to senior management in Chapter 23.

Tactic #4: If All Else Fails, Find Another Job (If Possible)

Meanwhile, protect yourself and your career; look elsewhere for a job where you can excel in a company that offers a good work environment and fair treatment.

Tactic #5: Whatever You Decide, Emerge a Winner

Maura met with me and invited me to a meeting with her attorney to discuss her situation. She'd faced several grueling depositions and countless requests for documentation entailing copious amounts of business records to prove she'd created and owned the material her former employee had pirated.

MAURA FELT DRAINED and ready to drop her lawsuit. Her attorney argued, despite Stuart's fiery bluster, that Maura had both right and the law on her side. He also told her that Stuart had filed a nasty countersuit, which, if she dropped her suit, might result in Maura paying money to Elliott.

I knew Maura's personal history and what it cost her to endure this legal firestorm. I told her I wanted her to emerge the victor, whatever decision she made, whether that meant dropping her lawsuit or proceeding with it, and winning, or, if she lost, winning because she had stood up for herself.

In our meeting, I asked Maura what spiritual base she relied on. To our surprise, she, Ted, and I learned we all described ourselves as born-again Christians.

With their permission, I quoted three sections from the Bible: Romans 8:31, "If God is for us, who can be against us? Who can do anything to me? He is my rock"; Ephesians 6:14, "Stand your ground, putting on the belt of truth and the body armor of God's righteousness"; and John 8:32, "And the truth will set you free."

I explained what I told others in workplace battles with scorched-earth bullies: that they might lack the firepower to defeat these bullies by themselves and might be best off leaving the field of battle, unless they could bring additional firepower to bear. Generally, this meant enlisting aid from a senior executive, the chief executive officer, the HR director, or the board of directors.

I said the decision was Maura's, and that she appeared to have a committed and competent attorney, a just cause, and her faith on her side. I added that I'd support her no matter what, and suggested that she consider what it would mean to her if she could transform the baggage of fear she'd carried from childhood.

Maura called both her attorney and me the next day to say, "Game on."

At trial, Stuart attacked her mercilessly. Maura practiced breathing, alternate focus, and putting on her game face (see Chapters 5 and 6). She later told me that these strategies carried her through her initial morning testimony and the first three afternoon hours of Stuart's cross-examination. It also helped that her attorney and a best friend had helped her rehearse how to answer attacking questions.

As the afternoon cross-examination dragged on, Maura said she felt herself melting down; she began to see an image of her brother standing immediately behind Stuart. "It was as if they became one and I was going back in time. I could feel myself lose my train of thought. I kept sipping water and trying to breathe, but nothing was working. I felt that familiar defenseless feeling."

DURING THE FINAL moments of cross-examination, Stuart asked Maura a crucial question, which, if she flubbed it, might lose her the case. Maura appeared to freeze; stuttering, she gave a confusing answer. When it seemed to Ted that all was lost, the judge leaned over and said, "Ms. Luden, do you mean to say _________ ?"

Ted said that in that moment he felt a courtroom miracle take place in front of his eyes. Maura turned toward the judge, nodded, and said, "Yes, that's exactly what I meant to say."

Stuart reared up to his full height, standing immediately in front of Maura, and shouted out his question again. In response, Maura answered, "What the judge just said."

Furious, Stuart sat down and muttered angrily, "No further questions for *this* witness."

In the judge's ruling, he described Maura's testimony as credible and her former employee's version as "not so credible." The judge referred the matter to mediation. The result: Her former employee paid all Maura's legal bills and agreed he would no longer use her materials.

Like Maura, you may discover you need more firepower than you possess to defeat a scorcher. In Maura's case, she had a committed attorney, the judge, and faith in God aiding her. Even a scorcher attorney realizes that judges rule the courtroom. Regardless of the outcome, if you stand up for yourself, you may win the fight even if you appear to lose it. By taking a stand or making the decision, "I can leave this job," you overcome the fear you were carrying. If this happens, the scorcher has done you a favor.

Your Turn: Where Are You Now?

If you have not encountered a scorcher, imagine what it would be like if you had, and answer the following questions accordingly.

1. Have you dealt with a scorcher? In what ways did the scorcher threaten you?
2. How did the scorcher's behavior affect you? What led you either to do battle with the bully or to back down?
3. What tactics (Chapter 9) did your scorcher employ?
4. What traps (Chapter 7), if any, did you fall into?
5. How did the scorcher's behavior affect others, and how did they act around the bully?
6. Maura initially gave Elliott several chances. What led her to do so? Do you believe that Elliott was a bully, and that Maura fell into bully trap #1, denial?
7. In your real-life situation, how did the scorcher's behavior affect morale and productivity?
8. What did you and others do to cope? What worked? What didn't?
9. Do you currently fear retaliation from a scorcher? If so, create objective documentation outlining what's occurring and store your notes off-site. By objectively recording the facts, you move them from your head onto paper where you can look at them more objectively.

   You'll also have the ammunition you may need. Effective documentation gives only the facts, without your subjective statements or emotions. If you write the facts correctly, anyone who reads them draws the same conclusions you do.
10. What actions did Maura take that led to her eventual success?
11. Have you ever been in a bully battle in which your personal history rose up and made it even harder to handle the situation? What did you learn from that?
12. What are your thoughts about the ways in which facing down a bully allows you to transform old fear baggage?
13. What advice would you give to someone who faces a scorcher?

14

DEFUSING THE SILENT GRENADE

The most courageous act is still to think for yourself. Aloud.

—COCO CHANEL

MIKE COWED MOST of his staff. He also knew how to handle those like Mitch who fought back reactively. In Cynthia, he met his match.

A tall, African American woman, Cynthia waved off those who warned her against coming to work for Mike. "He flies into rages," they said. "It's like working in a prison camp."

"I've raised four sons, all of whom thought they were God's gift to women," replied Cynthia. "I know how to deal with aggressive, entitled bullies."

Mike didn't appear to notice Cynthia during her first two weeks on the job. She observed how her coworkers cowered when Mike approached, but he left Cynthia alone. In her third week, during an all-staff meeting, Mike asked Cynthia a question about a report she'd prepared. Those listening knew Mike's question meant he didn't like the report's conclusions. Neither did he like Cynthia's answers. "Are you sure?" he yelled, starting to froth at his mouth.

"Oh, boy," muttered a man seated next to Cynthia. "Just offer to recheck your math."

Cynthia stared back at Mike. "I am sure. I wouldn't submit something I wasn't sure of."

"You get your big, fat, black ass back to your desk after the meeting and check it again. I don't expect to see numbers like this!"

"My what? What did you say about my body?"

"Your fat, black ass!" Mike screamed, losing control totally.

On her lunch hour, Cynthia visited the Human Rights Commission and filed a formal complaint. She identified nine witnesses to Mike's verbal attack, stressing that he'd screamed "black ass" twice at her. Cynthia told the commission that no other African American employees worked for Mike.

Mike flew into a rage when he received the commission's paperwork in the mail. Moments later, the commission's investigator called him to schedule a conversation. Mike blasted the investigator, yelling, "I'll call her anything I d--- well want to!" Mike immediately fired Cynthia, calling her an entitled b---- and saying she'd rue the day she had met him. Cynthia then amended her complaint to include a charge of retaliation.

Hefty legal bills and the commission's formal ruling against Mike convinced him that while he ruled his company, he didn't rule the regulatory agency. The commission didn't consider Mike's equally bad treatment of Caucasians and men a defense of the sexist and racist language he'd aimed at Cynthia. The commission's formal ruling ordered Mike to attend a four-hour discrimination, retaliation, and diversity training session and to pay Cynthia $10,000.

Although those who continued working for Mike feared he'd take his fury out on them, they noticed the reverse. Mike would start yelling, then catch himself, reconsider his words, and look around furtively to see who was watching.

Silent grenades (grenades) like Mike feel they're a breed apart from ordinary people. They rule because others fear their tirades and aren't sure what might set off the next explosion. When others deny grenades the power and control they insist on as rightly theirs, they rage; sometimes they appear crazed enough to do anything

Those who work for or around grenades monitor everything they say or do to avoid triggering an explosion. Grenade bosses employ a reign-of-terror management style. Those around them soon learn that reason or other efforts to calm grenades fail because past relationships and logic mean little to these tyrants. Because grenades delight in dominating any arena they occupy and lack a conscience, they prove exceptionally fierce opponents.

HOW TO PERMANENTLY SILENCE SILENT GRENADES

Grenades rule by intimidation. If you fear them and cower, you play their game and they win. If you fight, you again play their game, and they have more experience playing it than you.

What works? Standing up to them. Grenades lose sight of the fact that laws, regulatory agencies, and senior managers who take a clear look at what's going on rule the day—not the grenade.

In Cynthia, Mike had met a force larger than himself. Give a silent grenade an inch out of fear and he becomes your ruler. Monitor yourself and you create an uneasy stalemate yet work in fear. Document what the grenade is doing and find a regulatory body or a senior manager willing to step in, and you have a strategy that can work to silence your grenade.

Your Turn: Where Are You Now?

If you have not encountered a silent grenade, imagine what it would be like if you had, and answer the following questions accordingly.

1. Have you dealt with a silent grenade? What cues warned you of an imminent explosion?

2. What tactics (Chapter 9) did your grenade use?
3. How did the grenade's behavior affect you? What led you to do or not do battle with that grenade?
4. Did you fall into any bully traps (Chapter 7)?
5. How did the grenade's behavior affect others and how did they act around the grenade?
6. How did the grenade's behavior affect morale and productivity?
7. What do you wish your organization's senior management had done? What did they do? If they didn't act, what was the result of their inaction?
8. What did you do to cope? What did others do to cope?
9. If you currently feel threatened by a grenade, start your documentation, and file it off-site. Chapter 22 outlines how to write effective documentation and how to bring information forward to upper management.
10. What worked? What didn't?
11. What will you do differently in the future if you encounter a grenade?
12. What advice would you give to someone facing a grenade?

15

SEEING THROUGH THE SHAPE-SHIFTING MR. HYDE

Courage is contagious. When a brave man takes a stand, the spines of others are often stiffened.

—BILLY GRAHAM

PETER, A SLIM, almost handsome man with a receding chin, shrewd foxlike eyes, and a penchant for expensive suits, considered himself a man on the fast track. "I'm in line to be the CEO of my new corporation," he lied to those who joined him for drinks after work, a group whose faces changed every six months, given that Peter never kept "friends" for long.

The truth lay elsewhere. Every one to two years, Peter took a new job. Once in the new position, he crowed to those he left behind about his status and the perks he planned to enjoy, but, at his new job, he initially adopted a low-key persona.

Peter excelled at office politics and soon bonded with his immediate supervisor, Jim, a round-faced, gullible man. Peter presented a deferential, obsequious facade to Jim and other senior executives. He learned their birthdays and the names of their children. He took care to stop in their offices at least once a week to discover ways in which he could make himself valuable to them, whether by letting them know what he'd heard on the office grapevine or by enthusiastically offering to help them out in small ways.

If they allowed it, Peter "friended" those higher-ups on Facebook or attempted to link with them on LinkedIn. If they accepted, he made sure to notice the groups they connected with, and joined them. When Peter discovered Jim's manager, Steve, frequented LinkedIn's *Harvard Business Review* forum, Peter joined this discussion group, and made it a point to "like" each of Steve's posts. When another group member challenged one of Steve's posts, Peter launched a resounding defense of Steve's presentation.

Peter revealed a less pleasant persona to his peers, showing them his "claws" if they got in his way. He sneered at their accomplishments and belittled their abilities. He "forgot" to provide them promised updates and feigned apologetic misunderstanding of mutual commitments, turning those forced to collaborate with him into nervous wrecks when deadlines loomed. He took so long to provide coworkers with requested information that they regretted asking him, and soon left him alone.

A master of spin, Peter insisted any failure lay at others' feet, and he made any who criticized him, calling him "slippery" or "deceitful" to Jim, appear to be paranoid, jealous twits. When Jim mentioned these accusations to Peter "for his own good," Peter threatened the complaining coworkers, "Don't get in my way and don't cross me again. If you do, you'll lose, not me."

Shape-shifter bullies, as fictionally depicted as Dr. Jekyll and Mr. Hyde, "kiss up" and "kick down." They steal credit for others' efforts and stab in the back those who get in their way. Their agenda is their own success, and they work toward it, regardless of the cost to others. Supervisors or colleagues taken in by their Dr. Jekyll facade or their flattery soon learn that the shape-shifter's cooperative approach and ostensibly admiring gaze can evaporate like the mist on a hot summer morning.

REAL-WORLD TACTIC THAT WORKS

You may fall into bully trap #1 if you work with a shape-shifter. It's hard to believe that the "nice" person you see masks an evil twin. You and others tend to give a new colleague the benefit of the doubt, thinking, "I'll wait; maybe I'm misreading the situation."

Once you realize what you're up against, you face a second battle, which is how to convince others, particularly those who can do something about the problem, that the seemingly "great" employee is creating havoc. When explaining situations like this, we tend to present our opinion rather than objective facts. This never works, as those in charge wonder if we've reached the right conclusion. We need to learn how to provide "just the facts" so that others can draw the same conclusion based on facts, not opinions or some other bias. For example, if you tell your supervisor, "He terrified me," your supervisor may wonder if you are exaggerating. Instead, if you provide a factual accounting of events, you ensure that your supervisor reaches the correct conclusion. For example, you might say, "He stood over me while I sat at my desk and screamed I was a detestable b----; then he shook his fist in my face. Later, the receptionist told me that she heard him yelling three offices away."

Don't Go It Alone, Recruit Support

If you can enlist the support of a human resources professional or a senior executive, you can employ other approaches, such as a 360° review or an employee survey, to reveal the shape-shifter's true nature. Both strategies provide those who fear the shape-shifter's "claws" a confidential method for voicing their concerns.

A 360° review surveys seven to eleven individuals about a manager or professional and asks questions such as "What can you tell me about how this individual handles conflict?" and "How would you describe this individual as a leader?" A third party neutrally compiles the responses, edits out any "singular" comments so that all views presented are corroborated, and summarizes the results in the reviewer's own words to protect the anonymity of the participants. Chapter 26 provides additional information detailing what 360° reviews offer organizations when dealing with bullies.

Ultimately, these "how do we convince the powers-that-be what's occurring?" strategies were needed to counter Peter's shape-shifting behavior. Peter's boss, Jim, did not see Peter's political maneuvers even when they came straight at him. Although Peter ran over him like a freight train, Jim always thought the best of everyone and defended Peter to staff members who saw Peter's other side.

AFTER JIM SHARED that he had a less-than-solid relationship with Steve and others in the corporate office because they wanted a "shaker and mover" type and didn't value Jim's "team-building" style, Peter cultivated his relationship with Steve. In addition to his LinkedIn efforts, Peter called Steve with pseudo-legitimate questions, each time claiming, "I wanted to ask Jim but couldn't find him anywhere."

Peter also regularly sent Jim entrepreneurial emails, blind copying Steve. Each email began, "I know you've said this isn't a good time to launch a new initiative, but here's a way I think we can increase our revenue." Naively, Jim always stopped in Peter's office when he got one of these emails, saying, "Peter, any time's a good time. Let's flesh this out." Soon, Steve questioned whether Jim worked his full forty hours, and warned others in senior management that they might lose the "up and coming" idea guy, Peter, if they didn't "light a fire" under Jim.

Eventually, Steve called Peter and asked, "Tell me the truth. Does Jim work full-time?" Peter said, "I hate to say this because I like the man, but you can never find him."

"Does he encourage your ideas?"

"He likes the way things are."

Two weeks later, Steve fired Jim and named Peter acting supervisor.

That's when two of Peter's former coworkers sought me out. "What can we do?" they asked. "Jim wasn't perfect but he was fair and cared about us. Peter is two-faced, a bully who cares only about himself. He steals credit for other people's ideas and he takes out anyone who gets in his way or dares complain about him."

"If he becomes the new manager, either we'll be forced to leave or he'll find trumped-up reasons to fire us. We have kids and house payments, and we can't afford to take Peter on and lose our jobs."

I suggested they document the facts and present them to Steve, The next day they called me and said, "It's too risky. Peter asked where we'd gone yesterday for our 'extended' lunch hour. He smells something's up. We're going to keep our heads down and our noses clean."

I empathized with them, so because I had a LinkedIn connection with Steve myself, I called him. I explained I had heard of management changes in the Anchorage office and wondered if he'd be interested in a 360° review of any promising candidates. Steve grabbed hold of the idea, thinking the 360° review results would showcase Peter's talents to other senior managers who had questioned giving a plum management position to the relatively unproven Peter.

Although my company conducts these reviews, I suggested that Steve's corporate Human Resources staff conduct the review. I didn't want the fact that two employees had consulted with me to be perceived later as creating bias. More important, I worried that if Peter lost his promotion, he'd try to find out what led to his review and retaliate against the employees who had sought me out.

I told Steve, "If you conduct the review internally, your HR staff can provide Peter the follow-up coaching he needs to be a success." Steve elected to have two managerial candidates reviewed, Peter and a manager who worked in another branch. The other manager had been in the company for three years.

PETER HIMSELF SELECTED those to be interviewed and picked neither of the two individuals who'd visited me. Peter also met with each of his employees, who called these meetings "pepper sessions," because Peter "ground them up." He acted as if his being named manager was a "done deal" and explained he'd evaluate each employee on important criteria such as "allegiance." When asked to elaborate, Peter explained he'd always shown loyalty to his supervisors and expected the same from anyone who wanted to work for him.

Peter added that he believed the HR representative would give him a detailed accounting of the 360°'s results because she would realize that he needed specifics to manage effectively.

Morale plummeted. Employees dreaded what might happen if the company confirmed Peter as manager. As you might expect, the 360° review revealed Peter's two faces. Many rated Peter zero on the review's zero-to-ten leadership effectiveness scale. Several employees described Peter's communications as threatening. Three employees stated that many would resign were Peter appointed manager.

These results shocked Steve. When he called Peter to let him know he wouldn't become manager, Peter announced, "I feel betrayed by you." HR warned the new manager she might expect trouble from Peter, but Peter left for greener pastures.

Your Turn: Where Are You Now?

If you have not encountered a shape-shifter, imagine what it would be like if you had, and answer the following questions accordingly.

1. What would you have done if you worked with Peter?
2. Do you work with a shape-shifter?
3. How does your shape-shifter fool others? What warning signs

do others ignore? What leads them to ignore these warning signs?

4. How long did it take you to realize you worked with a shape-shifter?
5. If you worked with a shape-shifter, how did you convince others to believe your view of him or her?
6. What tactics (Chapter 9) did the shape-shifter use?
7. What traps (Chapter 7) did you or others fall into?
8. How did the shape-shifter's behavior affect morale and productivity?
9. How did the shape-shifter's behavior affect you?
10. How did the person's behavior affect others?
11. What did you or others do to cope? What worked? What didn't?
12. What will you do differently in the future?
13. What advice would you give to someone facing a shape-shifter?

PIERCE THE FACADE; TOPPLE THE NARCISSIST

The small Hitlers are around us every day.

—ROBERT PAYNE

PAULINE INITIALLY IMPRESSED the clinic's employees with her "vision" for what the clinic could become and her "I've got it all together" persona, but many grew to despise her.

Even though head nurse Molly never complained about Pauline's treatment of her to other employees, the stories flying across the clinic's grapevine made it clear that Pauline had gunned for the popular, highly respected Molly from day one. When Molly resigned ten months before her planned retirement date, several employees wept. Pauline hadn't expected this; she'd thought she'd made it clear that Molly's antiquated ways got in the way of progress.

The other staff members soon saw the truth behind Pauline's smoke screen, observing that her arrogance didn't stem from confidence but from a conviction that "there is only one way to do things—my way," and that her sense of entitlement hid a lack of accomplishment.

Employee after employee gave notice. Without head nurse Molly to buffer them, the experienced nurses left first, heading for better positions in local hospitals and competing medical clinics. Several first tried to talk with Pauline, out of loyalty to the clinic, but were told "Don't let the door hit you in the rear."

Those remaining hoped the physicians would notice the continuing exodus and ask questions, not realizing that Pauline had warned them to expect employee "fallout" as she "cleaned things up." Pauline herself conducted exit interviews with departing employees and advised each of them that if they wanted a good reference, she expected them to "watch their mouths." Most did.

When the clinic's IT manager resigned without notice after suffering through Pauline's blistering public attack on his competence, the managing physician contacted Pauline. "He's from the dark ages in network technology," Pauline assured the physician. "I gave him every chance, but he wasn't willing to grow with us. Here's the résumé of his replacement; this is a man I trust and what we need to move forward."

"We heard from two staff members, but couldn't quite believe, that you publicly shamed him," said the managing physician with a worried frown.

"Of course I didn't," insisted Pauline. "Modern leadership emphasizes being open and transparent. I spoke candidly to him about what we needed to do to move forward, which was something I wanted everyone to hear and learn from. Give me the names of those gossips."

"But . . . ," stuttered the conflict-averse managing physician.

"If you want me to run a successful practice for you, I need to manage bad behavior," Pauline insisted, persuasively. "It's workplace cancer."

"If you put it that way."

"I do," said Pauline.

The news that the managing physician had given Pauline the names of the two employees who spoke to him swept through the clinic like a wildfire.

What Pauline hadn't told the managing physician was that she wanted to replace the IT manager with someone she "trusted" to keep her informed of what the other employees said in emails. Like other narcissist bullies, Pauline had an entourage of sycophants and hired them as soon as possible when she moved to a new company. These yes-men and women knew how to stroke Pauline's ego in return for high-paying positions in which little real work was expected of them, if they kept Pauline happy. Soon, these toadies occupied key positions throughout the clinic.

REAL-WORLD TACTICS THAT WORK

When you're up against narcissist bullies, you can use the chinks in their armor to take them out.

Tactic #1: Find Their Weak Spots and Exploit Them

First, narcissists crave the limelight. Their hackles go up immediately when others receive praise or attention. This means they gun for popular individuals like Molly, and, if they take on the wrong individual, they bite off more trouble than they can chew.

Second, narcissists can't take criticism or any comments that challenge their self-esteem. When she initially came aboard, Pauline enjoyed the employees' admiration while Molly handled employee problems and took the brunt of their subsequent unhappiness. When Pauline became the clinic's sole administrator, she found herself the target of employees with gripes.

Third, narcissists manipulate everyone. Sooner or later, either someone with the power to fight back figures out she's been "had" and retaliates or those manipulated compare notes and realize what's going on. Narcissists, who expect others to idolize them, become enraged when their cover is threatened.

Tactic #2: Collect Information; Build a Solid Case

THESE VULNERABILITIES LED to Pauline's undoing. Gretchen, the low-key, deceptively mousy-looking woman who ran the clinic's accounting and billing department, had welcomed Pauline into the clinic. Pauline saw Gretchen as someone she could exploit, and cultivated this relationship. When Molly retired, Pauline took Gretchen out to lunch and told

Gretchen she planned to promote her now that the clinic was "mine, all mine."

Pauline's glee disturbed Gretchen, as had Molly's premature departure and the continuing employee exodus. Unsure about voicing her concerns, Gretchen prompted Pauline to talk about her "vision." Like other narcissists, Pauline enjoyed talking about herself.

Diligent and inquisitive by nature, Gretchen unobtrusively dug into Pauline's past. She learned Pauline had left two prior medical practices on bad terms. Gretchen began patiently collecting information from current and former employees, promising to keep who said what confidential. To each of them she said, "We built this clinic. We're acting as if this reign of terror is our new lot in life. Do we want it to go on this way?"

Gretchen prepared a spreadsheet for the physicians that contrasted employee turnover prior to Pauline's rise to power with turnover after she assumed sole control. She presented it to the managing physician late one afternoon on a day Pauline had left early.

He hurriedly called a meeting of the physicians. Gretchen's spreadsheet shocked the physicians, who hadn't put together the extent of the employee exodus. While each physician had been aware that one or two nurses and several front desk workers had quit, none of them had realized the total number of nurses, lab technicians, admitting clerks, and other support professionals who'd resigned. Pauline had instead focused the physicians on the "superstars" she'd brought aboard.

Without mentioning names or specifics that would reveal her sources, Gretchen also provided examples of what departing employees privately stated as their reasons for leaving. Gretchen begged the physicians to avoid outing her to Pauline and admitted that she was close to resigning herself. She also gave them an Internet-garnered description of a narcissist, noting she'd circled phrases she'd personally observed in Pauline, including grandiosity, inability to take criticism, salesmanship, self-absorption, and fury when others saw through their cover.

The physicians then met with Pauline and asked her questions. Pauline, unaccustomed to their scrutiny, flew into a rage, and accused them of being weak-willed children.

After Pauline stalked out, the physicians admitted to each other that they'd been bedazzled by Pauline and had shut their eyes and ears to the damage she'd inflicted on employee morale. They hired a consultant to conduct an independent employee survey and exit interviews with former employees. The consultant's report, along with legal advice, led the physicians to give Pauline a severance package in exchange for leaving.

Tactic #3: Don't Be Blinded; Be Aware of Warning Signals

When hiring managers ask me how to avoid hiring a narcissist, I suggest detailed reference checks, which reveal bridges burned and ashes scattered. Narcissists leave a trail. When interviewers find themselves dazzled by an applicant, they need to ask themselves if the applicant takes all the credit for a past organization's success, or shares it with others. They can ask applicants to describe a situation in which they've demonstrated teamwork. Narcissists can't, and instead talk about their own extraordinary effort. They show disrespect for others and blame others for problems rather than taking responsibility.

Your Turn: Where Are You Now?

If you have not encountered a narcissist, imagine what it would be like if you had, and answer the following questions accordingly.

1. Have you worked with narcissists?
2. How did they show their preoccupation with themselves?
3. How did they demonstrate their arrogance and their devaluation of others?

4. How did they show their sense of entitlement to do whatever they wished?
5. How did they demonstrate their tendency to hold grudges or their sensitivity to slights?
6. How did their behavior affect you?
7. How did their behavior affect others?
8. How did their behavior impact organizational morale and productivity?
9. What did you or others do to cope? What worked? What didn't?
10. Have you seen a narcissist attack another individual who got too much credit or attention? What happened?
11. Have you met someone who double-talked as well as Pauline, looking good on the surface despite rottenness underneath? How did you figure it out?
12. Although Pauline temporarily took her "throne" with her retinue in place, Gretchen toppled her. What characteristics did Gretchen show that allowed her to succeed? Which of those characteristics do you share?
13. Have you ever worked alongside a narcissist who dazzled others with his/her tinsel?
14. What advice would you give to someone else facing a narcissist?

TAKE DOWN THE RHINO BEFORE IT CHARGES

Success is not measured by what you accomplish but by the opposition you have encountered and the courage with which you have maintained the struggle against overwhelming odds.

—ORISON SWETT MARDEN

WHEN KRIS, A LEAN, red-headed woman with slate-gray eyes, took over the Alaska branch office of a Texas-based contracting company, she knew Don would present a major challenge. Not only did Don, a craggy-faced giant, openly share his "women don't belong in the field" opinions with anyone who'd listen, but he also expected star treatment.

The senior executive gave Kris her marching orders, "We expect you to corral Don. We don't want to lose him, but we can't afford him acting like an oil field Michael Jordan."

On her first day, Kris held a managers' meeting. Don failed to show. "Thumbing his nose," she thought. After the meeting, she sent Don a meeting request message. He didn't respond.

Kris's temper simmered as she reviewed her options: wait him out or go to his office. She marched toward the elevator, thinking "All right, showdown at the O.K. Corral."

REAL-WORLD TACTICS THAT WORK

Authoritative, forceful, mean-spirited wounded rhinos like Don count on pushing other people's buttons. If their targets react, the domineering rhinos charge and gore. Don had counted on Kris coming to his office and Kris almost fell into his trap.

Tactic #1: Launch a Preemptive Strike

INSIDE THE ELEVATOR, Kris caught sight of her clenched jaw in the mirrored wall. She pushed the button for the first floor, exited the building, and went to lunch. After lunch, she headed to one of the work sites Don managed.

As she drove up in her red 2015 Mini Roadster, three guys on a smoke break outside the building looked over as she exited her car. One gave her a long wolf whistle. "Gentlemen," Kris asked authoritatively, "is that how you greet the new branch manager?"

"Oh, s---," muttered one.

"What the hell?" said another.

"Indeed," announced Kris, "Call everyone into the lobby, right now, for a meeting."

Within six minutes, twenty men had assembled. "My name is Kris Williams and I wanted to meet you. In the next four weeks, I'll visit every Alaskan job site. I want to see firsthand what's happening in the field and give you a chance to put a face to a name. I have three initiatives, which you'll hear about in the coming months. None of them, however, is as important as safety. We've had two lost-time incidents in the last three months, and that's two too many. Any questions?"

A murmured "No" swept through the crowd.

"Thank you, gentlemen. I'll let you get back to work." As Kris finished, Don roared up in his Jeep and stomped through the lobby doors. The men saw his storm cloud face and headed for the elevator or the stairs.

"You visited my site," Don snapped through tight lips. "Without asking me?"

Kris rose to her full five-foot-six-inch height and calmly said, "You missed the managers' meeting and then apparently didn't see my meeting request. I figured you might be on-site."

Don looked hot enough to light a cigarette. "Lady, you don't need to be in the weeds."

"Devil's in the details, Don. There's a managers' meeting every Monday at 7 a.m. See you next week."

Natural dominators, rhinos control others through deliberate undermining, ill-temper, and calculated malevolence. Kris recognized Don's first two tactics: (1) disrespect evidenced by not showing up at the managers' meeting and (2) pushing her button by not responding to her meeting request.

She had no intention of letting Don run rampant. Her preemptive strike worked. She'd rattled him.

Tactic #2: Strategize and Act Before You're Gored

You'll recall Lexie faced a rhino named Jack who ruthlessly sabotaged her department in his battle to become executive director. Although the employees favored Lexie for the ED position, and she had earlier won many small private battles with Jack, the board wanted an ED who could handle Jack and chose an outside candidate.

What should you do if you face a rhino? Strategize and act before they charge, while they're still testing you. Once they've decided to take you out, rhinos gallop forward at thirty miles an hour, attacking with vengeance and giving no quarter. You need to take the high ground first, as Kris did on her first day—and each day after that—until Don gave her grudging respect.

Your Turn: Where Are You Now?

If you have not encountered a rhino, imagine what it would be like if you had, and answer the following questions accordingly.

1. Have you ever worked with or around a rhino? What did the rhino do and how did it affect you?
2. How did the rhino's behavior affect others?
3. How did their behavior affect morale and productivity?
4. What did you or others do to cope? What worked? What didn't?
5. What trap did Kris almost fall into?
6. What will you do differently in the future if you face a rhino?
7. What advice would you give to someone facing a rhino?

UNDOING A CHARACTER ASSASSIN'S WOUNDS TO YOUR REPUTATION

Man cannot discover new oceans unless he has the courage to lose sight of the shore.

—ANDRE GIDE

WHIPPET THIN AND DRESSED for battle in a tailored red suit, cream silk blouse, and red suede pumps, Heather wore her air of superiority as obviously as her strut proclaimed it. She cared about one thing, and one thing only, and that was Heather. She loved power and money. To her, that required establishing her reputation as the number one real estate agent in her city. Cassandra, long acknowledged as the city's leading authority on real estate matters, was the only obstacle in her way. Heather set out to destroy Cassandra's reputation among buyers, sellers, the media, and others in the real estate community.

Like many character assassins, Heather established a relationship with her target, fawning over Cassandra's accomplishments to her face while plotting to stick a reputation-slashing knife in her back.

Heather used LinkedIn to scope out Cassandra's connections, and linked to each of them, flattering them with complimentary introductions and inviting them to lunch. Most of them agreed. If they begged off, she delivered banana nut muffins and cappuccinos to their offices, first checking with their receptionists to determine whether they preferred caffeinated or decaffeinated beverages. Once Heather established a relationship with them, she passed along discrediting rumors about Cassandra at the same time as she pretended to admire her.

Heather worked her other connections to establish herself in the media spotlight. Her best friend from high school worked as a television reporter and featured her regularly in spots about real estate news.

Heather cultivated relationships with other women whose assistance she anticipated needing—a newspaper reporter, a public relations guru, and several leaders in the title and banking industry. These women met monthly and called themselves "the gang of seven." They dedicated themselves to helping each other realize their ambitions.

Heather attended every real estate or title insurance industry luncheon. Smiling, she quietly yet ruthlessly told agents about nasty remarks Cassandra supposedly made about them. Because these title and real estate agents saw Heather and Cassandra greet each other as friends in public, they swallowed Heather's stories, and cold-shouldered Cassandra.

Heather's friend, an IT guru, helped her create alternate Hotmail, Facebook, and Yahoo accounts she used to post defaming stories, allegedly from disgruntled buyers and sellers, about Cassandra.

A REAL-WORLD TACTIC THAT WORKS

Character assassins act without remorse, knocking others down so they can feel taller. Like many targets, Cassandra felt overwhelmed by the negativity swirling throughout her work community. When she attended industry functions, and individuals she had considered friends cold-shouldered her, she wondered what she'd done wrong. She cringed when she logged on to social media and saw postings criticizing her. At first, she wanted to retreat.

Launch a Counterattack

If a character assassin targets you, you can't run or hide. You can't afford to take assassins' gibes personally or signal that they've hurt you. To do so only emboldens them. Instead, you need to mount a counteroffensive.

When Cassandra called me, I suggested she take heart from the fact that her connections called to let her know what they'd heard instead of worrying about how much of the mud adhered to her reputation. More important, I urged her to reevaluate how she handled it when her connections called her about the derogatory rumors.

CASSANDRA BEGAN THANKING those who reached out to her and asked them where they'd heard the stories, which allowed her to trace many of them back to Heather.

Cassandra then hired a forensic computer specialist to trace the posts denouncing her on multiple Hotmail, Facebook, and Yahoo accounts. She learned Heather was behind many of them.

Cassandra decided to permanently douse the many brushfires Heather had started with a lightning strike. Several allies arranged for her to speak at an annual real estate convention. When Cassandra walked to the podium she noticed Heather and her cronies at a table immediately in front of the dais, apparently hoping their presence would intimidate her.

When Cassandra spoke, she talked about how she'd grown her career during lean years and how she'd honored those she'd learned from. While Cassandra spoke, Heather and her associates whispered to each other. Cassandra looked over their heads and maintained eye contact with the rest of the audience.

She then detailed the defamation of her character and professionalism that had occurred over the past months, and announced that she'd traced many of the posts and rumors to one person. When Cassandra then looked straight at Heather, the room fell silent.

"This is the greatest test of courage I've ever faced," Cassandra said. "To stand before you and let you know I almost gave up when things got ugly. If I had, you would not have seen me here today. But I am here. I stand before you and I stand on my record." One by one members of the audience stood to applaud, as Heather slid from her seat and fled the room.

Your Turn: Where Are You Now?

If you have not encountered a character assassin, imagine what it would be like if you had, and answer the following questions accordingly.

1. Has a character assassin ever targeted you? What did he or she do?
2. How did the behavior affect you? How did it affect others?
3. How did the behavior affect morale and productivity?
4. What did you do to cope? What did others do to cope? What worked? What didn't?
5. What did you learn from that experience?
6. What would you do differently in the future?
7. What advice would you give to someone facing character assassination?

19

THE NEWEST CHARACTER ASSASSIN: THE CYBERBULLY

The greatest test of courage on earth is to bear defeat without losing heart.

—ROBERT GREEN INGERSOLL

AFTER MAEVE LANDED THE sales manager position, she learned that a well-liked internal candidate had applied for the job but had been passed over. During Maeve's first week, the unlucky candidate and his closest friend resigned and took jobs with a competitor.

Then, without warning, Maeve's world exploded. Within a few days, Internet postings appeared accusing Maeve of landing the job by sleeping with her new boss, complete with explicit photos showing the back of a woman's head, her hairstyle resembling Maeve's. Other posts appeared, allegedly from Maeve's former coworkers, claiming Maeve's sales track record resulted from her sexual prowess.

Maeve felt dehumanized and helpless. She considered responding but felt any response might fan the flames. Her new boss and coworkers, however, believed that her lack of response indicated either weakness or an implicit acknowledgment of the truth of the accusations. Their initial warm welcome evaporated, and Maeve emotionally shivered in the frosty chill.

A high-tech lynch mob had successfully hacked Maeve's reputation.

Have cyberbullies gone after you? What causes cyberbullies to attack? What options do you have when they dump on you?

FREEDOM TO BULLY: THE MASK OF ANONYMITY

Pseudonyms and usernames allow cyberbullies to conceal their real identities on the Internet. This personal anonymity, coupled with membership in a faceless crowd, can create a situation in which some people sink to the lowest common denominator.

In one famous example, trick-or-treaters were invited to take candies left beside cash on a table in the front hall of a home. Eighty percent of those who arrived in groups and wore masks stole the money in contrast to 8 percent of the trick-or-treaters who arrived singly and without masks.

Absence of Social Constraints and Consequences

Online disinhibition, the loosening or complete abandonment of social inhibitions present in normal face-to-face interactions, can unleash needs and emotions that dwell below the surface. This emotional catharsis allows some Internet users to become less guarded and those with repressed anger to vent it online.

The fear of reprisal squashes unbridled personal attacks in face-to-face interactions. On the Internet, many character assassins voice inflammatory opinions freely, without worrying they'll lose a job or friend. Cyberbullies create far-reaching, even worldwide drama, generally free from consequences. If they go too far and provoke counterattacks, they can simply press reset and not log in again under that username or in that forum. They exit the scene even as the damage they've caused remains forever and may even go viral.

The Internet thus empowers character assassins and increases their sway and reach exponentially, leading them to attack without fear those they perceive as vulnerable.

False Belief That "It's Not Personal"

Because Internet users can't see each other, they don't always consider those they tweet or comment about as real people; this allows them to dissociate cruel remarks from the hurt their posts cause. A University of Haifa study revealed that those forced to maintain eye contact were half as likely to be hostile as those whose eyes did not meet.[1]

In one such instance, Tammy Blakey, the first female Continental Airlines pilot to fly the Airbus A300, experienced this depersonalization. Continental Airlines pilots and crew members used an Internet-based Crew Members Forum to learn their work schedules, receive flight information, and exchange views. When Blakey logged on, she found multiple posts describing her as a weak pilot who destroyed an engine, crashed a floatplane, and caused $250,000 in damage to a plane by flying it in a hailstorm.

Need to Create a Feeding Frenzy

Internet trolls sow discord by starting arguments or posting inflammatory comments with the deliberate intent of provoking emotional responses. They feed off others' comments. For them, the Internet's widespread, instantaneous access and their ability to inflict far-reaching damage with just one text, post, or email message proves irresistible.

REAL-WORLD TACTICS THAT WORK

Cyberbullies, like other character assassins, realize that repeatedly bombarding their target with one-sided information devastates the target and sways other people's opinions. However, you can take action against them.

Tactic #1: Launch a Counterattack

WHEN MAEVE STEPPED back and examined her situation, she realized that the two bullies weren't her biggest problem. Instead, because she hadn't responded to the cyberbullying barrage, her coworkers believed the allegations. Maeve decided not to take it lying down. She met with her new boss and asked him to convene a company meeting so she could set the record straight. He agreed; after all, his reputation was also at stake.

At the meeting she asked attendees to imagine that they'd accepted a job for which an internal candidate was considered a shoo-in and then to imagine that their reputation was trashed by anonymous postings, and that their only recourse was to take the high road or add fuel to the flames. "That's what happened to me, and, without any evidence that those postings are true, you've 'voted me off the island.' But how can I convince you that I'm telling the truth; all I can say is that those postings are vengeful lies." Maeve's genuine appeal melted the frosty chill, and one by one her new coworkers apologized for letting a cyberbully trash a new employee.

Tactic #2: Trace and Collect Evidence

If you receive threatening messages on your cell phone via text messaging, save the texts and trace the phone number through a reverse look-up directory or by searching for the phone number on Google, and then report the harassment to the mobile phone provider.

If cyberbullies haunt you on social media, print and save the posts as evidence and report the inappropriate messages to Internet service providers, which can trace and take action against posters who violate their abuse policy. Twitter, Facebook, YouTube, and Instagram all have online mechanisms for reporting abusive content. Twitter banned, for life, the users who sent graphic photos of a corpse to Zelda Williams, daughter of Robin Williams, after the comedian's tragic death. Most social media services and apps allow you to block individuals.

Obtain a Cyberstalking Injunction. If you suspect a specific individual of cyberbullying you, you can file a civil action against him or her. Your attorney can then use a civil subpoena to obtain the person's IP (Internet Protocol) address log-in record. If you need initial evidence to support the subpoena, a computer security specialist can track many cyberbully postings using the IP address. Some coworker cyberbullies foolishly use their employer's technology to go after you. In those cases, your IT manager can help you collect evidence.

If you obtain evidence that a bully has repeatedly used electronic communication to cause you substantial emotional distress through defamatory content, you may be able to secure a non-molestation order or cyberstalking injunction. A judge-granted ex parte cyberstalking injunction starts immediately. If you secure a final injunction, it lasts forever.

Protect Yourself; Call the Police. If cyberbullies or their posts threaten your safety, call the police. Cyberbullies who threaten your life step over the line into illegal activity. The police can track down even anonymous cyberbullies.

Tactic #3: Take Charge of Your Reaction

As you learned in Chapter 5, it's essential to act rather than react.

Responding to a cyberbully's attack may give the bully the attention he craves, and fuel further aggression. Never give cyberbullies what they want. Don't let them know they have your attention; block them and their messages.

If you delete offensive posts impulsively, you destroy evidence you may need later. If you lash out, you may spur the bully to create an infinite multitude of dummy accounts and post increasingly worse content.

Involve Your Employer. If you face coworker bullies, your employer may take your side, particularly if it pays attention to court rulings. When Tammy Blakey sued Continental Airlines, New Jersey's Supreme Court ruled that employers have "a duty to take effective measures to stop co-employee harassment when the employer knows or has reason to know" the harassment is "part of a pattern of harassment" in a setting "related to the workplace."

Attorney Lucinda Luke, an attorney specializing in labor and employment counseling and litigation, urges victims of employee cyberbullying to refer to "their company's employee handbook to determine if there are any policies prohibiting this kind of unacceptable behavior, workplace violence, harassment, and/or discrimination. Most employee handbooks address some or all of these issues and direct the employee to report this behavior so the employer can immediately investigate and correct it. If the bullying continues, alert your employer that the actions taken were not successful in stopping the bullying."

Sue the Bully or Your Employer. Continental pilot Blakey sued her employer for not taking action to protect her, winning $875,000 from a jury who agreed with her.

Tackle the Perception Battle. A bully's slander succeeds only when others believe it. Defend yourself proactively by ensuring that those you work with recognize your integrity and worth. Sun Tzu's military treatise, *The Art of War,* advises that a warrior best wins a war by being an individual no one wants to take on.

Like other bullies, cyberbullies can dish it out but can't take it. Don't let cyberbullies shame you into isolation. Connect with your friends and coworkers and ask them to participate in a counterattack, by blocking online aggressors, reporting hurtful messages to moderators, and creating posts supporting you.

Harness the power of technology yourself by creating a YouTube video that refutes the story being spread.

Close the Door. You can prevent the bully's attacks from reaching you by canceling all social media and personal email accounts. At work, your company's IT provider can show you how to permanently filter out unwanted messages, and you can open new accounts blocking the bully's emails.

The Employer's Duty. As Blakey's employer, Continental Airlines, learned, employers that allow employees to be cyberbullied have potential liability if the cyberbullying starts in the workplace. It often does. According to a recent survey, 48 percent of businesses permit all employees to "access social networking sites at work for non-business use."[2]

The Most Common Areas of Employer Liability

- Tweets, Facebook, or blog posts one employee makes about another that involve or escalate to harassment and originate in the workplace or spread into the workplace.
- Employees who cyberbully on work time, or use employer-provided computers or other technological resources when bullying.
- Employees who cyberbully on employer-sponsored social media such as the employer's Twitter, LinkedIn, blog, or Facebook page.

Devastated by attacks from a cyberbully? Take heart. Maeve talked to her coworkers. Tammy took legal action. Both prevailed.

Your Turn: Where Are You Now?

If you have not encountered a cyberbully, imagine what it would be like if you had, and answer the following questions accordingly.

1. How would a cyberbully's behavior affect you?
2. What could you do to cope?
3. It's more difficult for a cyberbully to destroy your workplace reputation if you've created a strong one. In what ways can you demonstrate your integrity and value in your workplace to handicap a cyberbully's ability to slander you?
4. What privacy protections do you have in place for your social media accounts? Each online vendor has guidelines for creating privacy settings. Act now to set up privacy protections on Facebook, Twitter, and other social media accounts to ward off potential assassins.
5. It's always better to respond strategically than to react. Prior planning makes this easier. Decide the first steps you'll take if attacked by a cyberbully. Will you print the offensive posts immediately? Make this decision now, before you're attacked and while your head is cool.
6. If you're a manager or a human resources professional, what actions will you take or recommend to protect your organization from liability and your employees from cyber-bullying? This is a good time to put in place an anti-bullying policy such as the draft one offered in Chapter 26.
7. What advice would you give to someone facing a cyberbully?

NOTES

1. Noam Lapidot-Lefler and Azy Barak, "Effects of Anonymity, Invisibility, and Lack of Eye-Contact on Toxic Online Disinhibition," *Computers in Human Behavior*, 28, no. 2 (March 2012): 434–443.

2. Proskauer, Social Networks in the Workplace Around the World, http://www.proskauer.com/files/uploads/Documcnts/Survey-Social-Networks-in-the-Workplace-Around the-World.pdf.

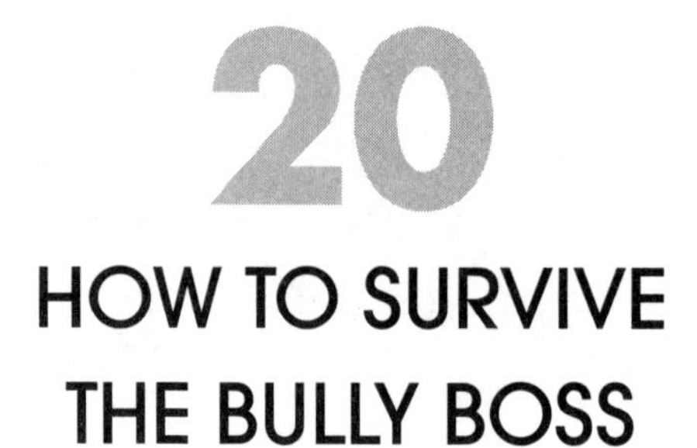

20 HOW TO SURVIVE THE BULLY BOSS

At the worst, if he fails, at least he fails while daring greatly, so that his place shall never be with those cold and timid souls who neither know victory nor defeat.

—THEODORE ROOSEVELT

WHEN NANCY ARRIVED AT her new job, prior to 8 a.m., she poked her head into the accounting manager's office. "Hi, I'm reporting for duty," Nancy said brightly.

"Whoops," responded Yvonne, "We don't pay overtime."

"I wouldn't charge overtime, I thought I'd just get to my desk and get a head start. I promise I won't sign in."

"I appreciate your enthusiasm, but if I let you upstairs," said Yvonne, biting off her words, "it's on my head."

"Okay," said Nancy, "I'll wait."

At two minutes before 8:00, she returned. Yvonne looked up and said "I'll take you up. You're required to be at your work station by 8 a.m. every day; however, you're not allowed to sign in until 8:00. Also, lateness is not allowed—not even a minute."

"Okay," said Nancy, as they headed upstairs. "Do you know when my boss gets in and if there's an orientation?"

Strain clearly showing on her face, Yvonne replied, "Our general manager prefers to orient you himself. He'll be in when he's in."

Nancy looked shocked.

"I'm sorry," said Yvonne, "It's just that Steve has certain rules and we don't question him."

"No problem. I'm sorry if I've overstepped."

After Yvonne left, Nancy turned her computer on, and was cleaning her desk drawers when she heard heavy footsteps.

A man stuck his head through her doorway, and in a deep, raspy voice snapped, "I'll see you, now."

"Yes, sir," Nancy said, hustling after Steve into his office. There were no chairs in front of Steve's desk, so she stood while he sat down, thudding into a giant, black leather chair.

"Pay attention, and you'll do well," declared Steve, without any welcoming preamble. "I expect eight hours' work for eight hours' pay. Phone numbers are to be repeated twice for accuracy. I expect total discretion. Plus, I don't like idiot questions."

"Yes, sir." Nancy shivered.

"I'm done," bellowed Steve, with obvious irritation.

Nancy fled back to her desk.

THE BULLY BOSS TURNS A JOB INTO A NIGHTMARE

Bully bosses chip away at their employees' self-confidence and potential with belittling comments. They demand instant and complete obedience. If you challenge the bully boss's opinions, or ask too many questions, the "I rule" boss reacts angrily, forcing you to back down and teaching you to keep your mouth shut.

Bully bosses dominate, exploit, and devalue their staff. Their idea of give and take is they take, you give. They ferret out your vulnerabilities and use them as ammunition. Even if you're used to standing up for yourself, you may find yourself outgunned and defeated.

Bully bosses rarely see themselves as bullies. Instead, they see employees and others as the problem, often saying things like "You've got to kick people to get them going" or "I'm yelling because they don't hear me unless I shout."

Bully managers live in a feedback vacuum because peers don't call them on their behavior, and subordinates don't voice concerns, fearing they'll be fired.

REAL-WORLD TACTICS THAT WORK

NANCY RECOGNIZED THE situation for what it was. She'd been married to a bully who'd died of a heart attack at fifty-six, but not before he'd flattened her self-esteem. She gritted her teeth and reminded herself that it took her three months to land this job.

She returned to her computer and plowed into the piles of work on her desk. Twice, Nancy knocked softly on Steve's door.

"What d'ya want?" he asked.

"I have completed letters for your signature."

"Well, bring them in!"

As Nancy handed them to him, she saw the plaque, "It IS my way or the highway, and the highway is right out front." She suppressed a smile. She couldn't have asked for a more "in your face" bully.

After her husband died, she'd sought out a grief counselor, who told her she needed to repair her self-esteem as well as grieve. Nancy realized quickly what she might gain from a short stint working for Steve.

Tactic # 1: Help Them Attain Their Goals

Bullies appreciate those who enhance their reputation and help them realize their ambitions. By supporting your boss you decrease the likelihood you'll be the victim of choice.

Tactic #2: Avoid Confronting a Bully Boss

DURING NANCY'S FINAL counseling session, she'd told the counselor, "I'm afraid to ever date again. What if I pick another bully?"

"You now have bully radar," the counselor assured her. "If you date someone who acts like a bully, you'll dump him. If you end up working with bullies, consider it practice in how to stand up to them."

"You mean fight them?"

"You can stand up to bullies without a fight. The trick is to not let them destroy your sense of well-being or force you to retreat."

As Steve blew by her desk on his way out to lunch, Nancy thought, "This guy may be my final exam in handling bullies without letting them trash my self-worth."

Nancy learned Steve's triggers and took great satisfaction in doing a better job than he expected. She kept her head down and worked hard. She sensed that Steve was trying to bury her in work so he could blow up when she cracked.

Don't challenge bully bosses by expressing your opinions or asking questions. Instead, if you can tolerate their arrogance, let them know what you admire about them and quietly go about doing what you think is right. Learn what triggers their anger so you can avoid setting them off.

Tactic # 3: Don't Expect Their Approval or Loyalty

Even if they temporarily treat you well, bullies' positive regard can evaporate in a nanosecond. Then, they'll turn on you no matter how much you've done. Bullies are guided by their own risk/reward radar. They pick on the weakest members of their team first; however, even if you don't fall into that category, you can't afford to threaten them. Instead, strengthen yourself, inwardly and outwardly, by developing an ally base.

Tactic #4: Use the Bully Boss's Interest in Their Favorite Person—Themselves

ONCE A DAY Nancy grabbed coffee from the break room and ate her sandwich at her desk. On her second week, she walked in on two coworkers she'd not met, who were betting on how long she'd last.

"Hi! Can I get a cut if I stay?" The two jumped. "So what odds are you giving me?"

"Ten to one that you won't last out the month."

"Has he always been this bad?"

"Ha!" one snorted. "You haven't seen anything until you've seen him in a rage." They heard heavy footsteps coming down the hall. All three scrambled out the door and back to their desks.

That night, Nancy began looking for a new job. Not wanting word to get back to Steve that she was job hunting, she omitted her new job from her résumé and used her maiden name, thinking it was time to legally change her name anyway.

Two months later, she lined up a new job. By then, she'd met and liked many of her coworkers. Several told her how surprised they were that she "wasn't a b----." The first man who made that comment said, "Your predecessor was. We all figured that was what it took to handle working that close to Steve."

Nancy wanted to do something for her coworkers before she left. She was getting out, but, in the tight job market, many of them were stuck working for Steve. Also, most of them liked their work, although not the oppressive environment.

As she'd suspected, Steve had put her through trial by fire and, because she'd handled it without faltering, now relied on her. While he barked at her occasionally, he often asked for her thoughts about one of his plans. Wisely, she always told him what she admired about whatever he proposed, and never voiced objections. Because she opened his mail, Nancy also seized the opportunity to put things into his mail stack she wanted him to see.

When she learned about 360° reviews, she sought out information and realized the potential benefits.

Generally, bully bosses have an inflated view of themselves, their leadership qualities, and how much their employees admire them—and they like having those views confirmed. If you work for a bully boss, consider what you appreciate about him or her and let the boss know it.

Bully bosses also desire information that they can use as ammunition to increase their control of their employees and organizations. As a result, they often accept a consultant's or human resources professional's suggestion to implement a 360° review. Sometimes, this neutrally gathered information can convince a bully boss to learn new ways of treating others.

Tactic #5: Document Your Boss's Behavior

If your bully boss runs your department rather than the organization, or reports to a board of directors, demonstrating the cost to the organization in morale, productivity, and turnover carries great weight. When you have enough documentation bring it to the chief executive officer or board chair's attention; it may convince them to rein in the bully.

Tactic #6: Know Your Legal Rights

While bully bosses may rule their organizations or departments, they don't rule the world. If your bully boss discriminates illegally against you and you're a member of a protected category based, for example, on your age, sex, race, or pregnancy, or a part of another statutorily protected group, seek help from your state's Human Rights Commission or from the federal Equal Employment Opportunity Commission.

If your bully boss lashes out at you because you've engaged in a protected activity, such as protecting your right to work in a safe workplace, document the situation and bring it to the attention of the relevant regulatory body. Chapter 27 provides a full list of the protected activities and categories that may help you take out your bully boss.

Tactic #7: Don't Let Your Bully Boss Steal Your Visibility

This is especially true if you've generated new, innovative ideas that may help you leapfrog past your boss in the organization's hierarchy. Establish credit for your ideas before a bully boss claims your work as his or her own.

Tactic #8: Besting the Bully Boss

ONCE NANCY KNEW she had another job lined up, she called a consultant on her personal cell phone and outlined the situation. "I have a tyrant boss—fifty-three people in this organization and one man makes their lives miserable. I'm thinking a 360° review would hold a mirror up to our boss."

"It does, better than almost anything else I know."

"Would it be possible to do one of these reviews and keep it confidential?"

"Everyone emails me their forms. They can do it from their home computers or another computer that's not part of your office network because anything that is sent from your network to an outside third party can be captured and reviewed. Or, I can send you fifty-three printed questionnaires, along with self-addressed stamped envelopes, and they can mail them to me confidentially."

"What if our boss asks you for them and recognizes people's handwriting?"

"You have my word I'll input the data and shred the original questionnaires."

"We have a plan."

The consultant provided a brochure along with the names of the largest companies for which she'd done 360°s. Nancy slid the information into Steve's stack of mail and placed the mail on Steve's desk.

"What the hell is this crap?" he asked her, fishing out the brochure on the 360° leader review.

"What, sir?"

"This stuff from some management consultant?"

"Oh," she said, as she took the brochure. "I've heard about these. A lot of Fortune 500 companies are using them, but only for their top leaders."

"Hrmh!" Steve grunted.

As she exited, she heard Steve making a call, and crossed her fingers.

Nancy handed Steve her resignation the day after she knew most employees had mailed in their questionnaires. As she had predicted, he fired her on the spot. "Thank you, sir," she said gaily. "I consider that an A."

Your Turn: Where Are You Now?

If you have not encountered a bully boss, imagine what it would be like if you had, and answer the following questions accordingly.

1. Have you worked for a bully? What bullying behaviors did your boss exhibit?
2. In what ways did this boss try to control or dominate you?
3. What other maladaptive behaviors did your boss exhibit?
4. What happened to your self-confidence when you worked with this boss?
5. In what other ways did your bully boss affect you?
6. Did your bully boss realize he or she was a bully?
7. Nancy helped her bully boss realize his goals; did you use a similar strategy?

8. Although Nancy didn't fight her bully boss, in what ways did she stand up for herself?
9. How did you strengthen yourself internally?
10. How have you found and used allies?
11. Were you able to access a member of the board of directors or a manager more senior than your bully boss to help you?
12. If you've been bested in the past by a bully, how could successfully handling a bully transform your life?
13. If you currently work under a bully boss, are there any regulatory agencies, such as the Human Rights Commission or the Department of Labor, that can help you? (Note: You will find more ideas in Chapter 27.)
14. How did your bully boss's behavior affect others?
15. How did the boss's behavior affect morale and productivity?
16. What did you do to cope? What did others do to cope? What worked? What didn't work or made things worse? What would you do differently in the future?
17. What advice would you give to someone who works for a bully boss?

21

HANDLING THE BULLY EMPLOYEE WITHOUT GETTING BURNED

Nothing is a waste of time if you use the experience wisely.

—AUGUSTE RODIN

EARLIER, YOU MET golden boy employee Geoff, who bullied his easy-going supervisor Adam from the day the senior manager promoted Adam instead of Geoff to a plum position. Because Geoff thought the job was rightfully his, he felt justified in treating Adam like trash. Conflict-averse Adam let Geoff push him around and usurp his role in staff meetings. Finally, Adam had had enough, and realized he had to act.

If you're bullied by someone who works for you, you may feel a special shame. After all, you could fire this employee—or so everyone else thinks.

Disciplining or firing a bully, as you may know firsthand, isn't always easy. Perhaps your bully employee has a talent your organization needs and, if you fire the bully, you might not be able to easily replace his skill set. The bully may have tenure or union protection. Maybe the bully is a member of a protected group due to his age, sex, race, or some other characteristic, and you're concerned that if you fire him you'll face an ugly lawsuit. You may fear that because the bully's coworkers have a different relationship with the individual who bullies you, they'll resent you for terminating someone they like. Conversely, you may employ a bully who treats you well but bullies his or her coworkers, and you find it hard to believe the stories they tell you.

Supervisors disciplining bullies often feel they've flown into a box canyon. The moment they start the disciplinary process, the bully fights back with everything he has, and the supervisor feels as if she'd been slammed straight into a granite wall.

Bully employees have multiple reasons for bullying supervisors and few qualms about fighting back when supervisors attempt to discipline them. Employees who consistently bully do so because bullying brings them success. They feel no remorse; in fact, they feel justified in their actions.

Employee bullies may lie, both to your face and about you behind your back. They regularly challenge what you say and your motivation for saying it. They often create an uproar in an attempt to make you back off or to topple you. They distort your actions to their coworkers, leading other employees to wonder why you are "so mean." They learn where you're vulnerable and press those buttons.

REAL-WORLD TACTICS THAT WORK

You can survive this, if you employ the following tactics when a bully employee has you tied in knots.

Tactic #1: Don't Play Nice—You Can't Afford It

As a supervisor, you need to lead and manage. Don't let bully employees "run the show" while you accommodate them with chance after chance. If you allow a bully to continue problem behavior unchecked, you let your other employees and yourself down.

Tactic # 2: Listen to Your Employees

If a staff member or members tell you another employee bullies them, listen. Many bullies kiss up and kick down. Don't assume that problem behavior you haven't personally seen or experienced doesn't exist.

Tactic #3: Don't Give a Bully a Bully Pulpit

No matter how large your workload, spend time connecting with your employees, so that you establish and maintain a good relationship and two-way communication with each worker. A bully employee who hopes to overthrow the supervisor spends considerable time cultivating covert relationships with coworkers, and then uses these to poison them against the supervisor. If your employees don't get to know you, they may believe your bully employee's misrepresentations of you.

Tactic #4: Protect Yourself Against Sabotage

Realize that your bully employee may try to undermine how senior managers view you. The bully may wait until you're out of the office, trump up an excuse to contact your manager, and say, "Ordinarily, I'd ask my supervisor this question but it's time-critical and I haven't been able to find him." A bully employee who plays this game regularly can successfully undercut how upper management thinks of you.

Tactic #5: Don't Delay—Assess the Situation and Take Action

ADAM ASKED HIS manager for a meeting and outlined everything that had happened since his promotion. He described his efforts to reach out to Geoff, and Geoff's undermining actions. He asked his boss's permission to meet with Geoff and handle the situation, even if it meant Geoff might quit.

"You've got it," Adam's boss said. Then he asked, "Has it occurred to you I could have selected Geoff instead of you?"

"Yes."

"Why do you think I picked you?"

"I don't know."

"That's part of the problem. I wanted an employee who could get along with others. You have those skills. You've also stepped up to every challenge you've encountered, except this one. Today's meeting is overdue."

Let truth and fairness guide you. Is it right that your bully employee be allowed to get away with his behavior? If not, decide what you need to do and do it. The bully may try to muddy the waters with trumped-up issues. Don't fall for his ruses.

Never "put off until tomorrow" when tackling a bully's bad behavior. While you're deciding whether or not to take action, your bully employee can damage morale and create a toxic environment for you or others. If you find yourself frustrated daily by the bully's misbehavior, find a senior manager, coach, or other individual who can help you develop and implement a game plan.

Remember, bullies test to see who runs the show, you or them. If they take advantage, and you initially allow it, and insist they "toe the line" only when you've "had enough," they'll retaliate fiercely to protect their power and privilege.

Although you need to act swiftly, take the time you need to reflect on the situation and to act wisely. Otherwise, your bully employee may use what you do to create a hostile environment or, if fired, might allege wrongful termination or initiate a lawsuit. Before you discipline a bully or any other employee, make sure you've clearly and specifically outlined fair expectations for your employee's performance and behavior. If the bully violates those expectations, promptly and fairly confront the situation.

HOW TO EFFECTIVELY CONFRONT A BULLY EMPLOYEE

AFTER HIS TALK with his boss, Adam blinked. What was it that had led him to let bullies like Geoff walk all over him? What was he scared of?

He took a long walk that night and asked himself those questions, as well as "Is it right that I allow Geoff to act the way he does?" "What is this situation doing to team morale?" and "As the supervisor, what should I be doing?"

Then he asked himself, "Do I want to continue to be powerless or do I want to rise to the challenge?"

The next morning, Adam called Geoff and asked to meet with him in his office. At first, Geoff put him off, protesting, "I'm really busy."

"It's a mandatory meeting."

"All right," Geoff drawled.

You'll know you're ready to confront the employee if you can answer yes to two questions:

1. Have you defined the problem behavior, your expectations, and the importance of meeting those expectations objectively and specifically?
2. Have you investigated and documented the situation? (Chapter 23 outlines how to write effective documentation.)

Begin by Setting the Stage

Let the bully know why you are having the discussion. For example, you could say, "I'd like us to have a productive discussion that results in improved performance and behavior. I'll be asking you questions in order to understand your perspective. Please feel free to ask me questions. My goal is that when we leave the room, we're on the same page."

With this start, you accomplish two outcomes. If you've incorrectly assessed your employee as a bully, you've created a positive start. If, however, he is a bully, your statement emphasizes that you consider yourself his equal. Later in the discussion you can affirm your supervisory status by adding, "It's important we come to an agreement," and then outlining the negative consequences the employee faces if he does not meet the standard you set.

Outline the Issue and Your Expectations

WHEN GEOFF ARRIVED forty-five minutes later, Adam said, "Geoff, I wanted you on the team."

Looking bored, Geoff snickered, "What team is that?"

"I don't any longer," Adam continued, ignoring Geoff's snide retort.

Geoff rolled his eyes, but Adam looked straight at Geoff, and then held out a one-page document.

"I've reviewed your actions since I received my promotion. I haven't called you on them. That's changing. Here's a list indicating the behavior I expect from you and every team member."

Geoff smirked, but didn't reach for the page Adam held out to him. "What is this garbage?"

"Your last chance. There's a place for you to sign at the bottom of the page."

Geoff reared up. "I'll walk."

"You'd rather walk than change?"

"That's right," snarled Geoff, hostility radiating from him like mist from a bog.

"That's too bad. I'm done putting up with your behavior."

Not all employee bullies are willing to go as far as Geoff did; some will respond by, at least, putting their own spin on the situation. Listen to what your employee says. Your bully employee may try to derail the discussion by angrily reacting. Don't lose your temper; instead, keep the discussion on track. Once you've heard the employee's perspective and taken it into account, you might say, "These are the expectations you need to meet."

You may want a third party, such as your organization's human resources officer, another supervisor, or a management consultant, to sit in on the meeting, either to help facilitate the discussion or to assist you by documenting what was and wasn't said.

WHEN ALL ELSE FAILS: TERMINATING A BULLY EMPLOYEE

GEOFF SLAMMED OUT of Adam's office and barged into their manager's office, angrily protesting the unfair treatment he'd just received from his "incompetent supervisor."

When the manager didn't rally to Geoff's defense, Geoff accused the manager: "You promoted the wrong person. And you never responded to my emails!"

"I saw them for what they were," the manager responded.

Geoff didn't ask the manager what he meant, but instead stormed out. He then hired an attorney who sent a threatening letter alleging constructive discharge (intolerable working conditions). Adam's manager responded by sending detailed documentation concerning Geoff's behavior after Adam's promotion. The company never again heard from Geoff.

If oral counseling doesn't work, fairness generally requires that you have a second, more formal, meeting, called a written reprimand, where, in addition to your oral discussion, the employee is given written documentation, which he must sign, enumerating the performance and behaviors he needs to achieve. Because the employee signs the reprimand, if you need to terminate him later, the bully can't say "I didn't know."

Questions to Ask Yourself Before Firing a Bully Employee

Courts require employers and supervisors to act in good faith and fairness when terminating employees, so to be certain you have, consider the following before taking any action:

- Have I required the same performance of the bully as I have required of other employees?

- Have I treated other employees with similar records the same way or differently?
- Have I warned the employee what action will be taken if his or her behavior and performance fail to improve?
- Do I have sufficient documentation to convince a neutral third party, such as a judge, jury, or regulatory agency, that this employee deserved to be fired?

While a bully employee may have pushed your buttons until you feel, "It's the bully employee or me that must go," never lose your temper. A supervisor who keeps his or her cool and is in the right can successfully manage, discipline, and even terminate a bully employee.

Finally, although supervisory disciplinary tools can help you manage a bully employee, your internal decision making plays an equally vital role. If you're one of the many supervisors who let a bully employee push you around, ask yourself, "What is it going to take for me to rise to the challenge?" Then, whatever it is, find it.

Your Turn: Where Are You Now?

1. Although you might not be a supervisor, the discussion in this chapter might have prompted you to consider the question "Why do I allow others to push me around?" What's your answer?
2. Do you supervise or work with a bully employee? What would your answer be to the question posed in this chapter, "What is it going to take for you to rise to the challenge?" Why is it so important for supervisors or managers to handle bully employees? How do they let themselves and their employees down if they don't?
3. Have you ever encountered an employee bully who poisoned coworkers against a supervisor? If you were the

supervisor at that time, what happened and how did you handle it? If you were an employee, were you swept along by the bully's actions or were you a bystander? If a bystander, what did you do?

4. Of all the guidance provided in this chapter, what did you find most helpful? Why?
5. If you know a supervisor facing a bully employee, consider taking a risk. Meet with the supervisor and explain what you learned from this chapter.

NINE ESSENTIAL STRATEGIES FOR CREATING YOUR GAME PLAN

Things don't happen, they are made to happen.

—JOHN F. KENNEDY

HAVING COME THIS FAR, you probably realize much about what led you to be bullied and how you can beat workplace bullies in your life. You've most likely turned some of those insights into commitments to yourself. In this chapter, I will show you how to formulate those commitments into goal statements and to develop your game plan.

By setting goals and creating plans, you have the opportunity to live your life by design rather than by default.

FORMULATE YOUR GAME PLAN

In this chapter, you'll set at least one goal and learn how to turn goal setting into goal achieving. If you've ever made a promise to yourself, only to watch your motivation fade and your dream evaporate, you know the importance of a defined plan.

Strategy #1: Set One Goal You'd Give Anything to Reach

Let yourself dream. A goal you really care about provides inspiration in the same way that the chance to win a tournament keeps an athlete performing without noticing how exhausted she is. What do you want to change in the way you handle bullies? For example, do you want to keep bullies from gaining an outpost in your mind? Or do you want to be able to stand up for yourself whenever someone assaults you verbally?

Write your goal on a piece of paper or enter it in your computer.

Strategy #2: Rev up Your Energy

Heading for a goal with partial energy is like driving forward with the parking brake on. Take your foot off the brake, let yourself feel excited, and power up your momentum by focusing on how you'll feel about yourself and your work life once you've achieved your goal.

Answering the following questions can help you focus on the benefits you'll get once you've achieved your goal:

- What will change for you at work? For example, will you enjoy coming to work every day again?
- What excites you about this goal?
- How might attaining this goal impact your career?

Strategy #3: Make Your Goal Real

Two popular New Year's resolutions, "I'm going to lose weight" and "I'm going to exercise more," often fail. Why? General goals rarely capture enough mental energy to power you all the way through to the finish line, given the occasional tackle or takedown. While goals such as preventing bullies from gaining an outpost in your mind or standing up to an angry, aggressive jerk's caustic comments may initially excite and inspire you, you won't always achieve lasting change unless you frame your goal more concretely.

You can do this by making your goals vivid, by setting time frames and targeted outcomes. A specific deadline gives your goal added punch. You may even decide the time is now and write your goal in "from this day forward" terms. An action verb or a target outcome such as "I'll lose six pounds by September 30" makes your goal definitive.

Here are two workplace bully examples:

1. From this day forward, I'll respond assertively to snarky attacks.
2. By September 15, I will have met with the chief operations officer and provided objective information concerning the ways in which my immediate supervisor bullies my coworker and me. By September 25, I'll have made a mental decision about what I'll do if my concerns are not addressed or the situation worsens.

Write/enter your goal with a time frame and a clear, targeted outcome.

Strategy #4: Visualize Your Goal

You can make your goal even more inspiring by creating an intense visual picture of what your goal means. Imagine the future, one in which you've achieved your goal. Allow yourself to fully feel the emotions you'll experience and to vividly picture how you'll look and act.

As a reminder, write/enter a few phrases that describe what you pictured in your mind.

Because keeping your goal in mind creates regular inspiration, you may want to mentally picture your goal each morning as you awaken and, again, just before you head to work.

Strategy #5: Make Sure Your Goal Is Realistic

Do you believe you can achieve your goal? If you are unsure during the goal-setting process, you weaken your chances of success. Occasionally, we trip ourselves up by formulating inspirational yet "out of reach" goals. If you've done this, redraft your goal in more attainable terms. Just as an overweight person might redraft "I will lose one hundred pounds this year" into a more realistic "I will lose nine pounds in the next three months," you might write "I will respond to snarky comments with statements like 'Pardon me?' or 'What is your point?'" rather than "I'll think quickly on my feet and be able to turn the tables on a bully's nasty comments with a humorous comeback."

By setting a realistic goal to which you can fully commit, you increase your chances of attaining your initial goal. Once you've attained your first goal, you can set an even more challenging one.

So, do you want to downsize your goal to a more realistic one? Or, can you commit 100 percent to your initial goal? If so, you're on your way.

Strategy #6: Design Your Strategies

Now that you've established your goal, what strategies might you use to achieve it?

For example, Adam might write, "I will sit down with Geoff within forty-eight hours and give him a list of my expectations for his future behavior." Or, "If Geoff targets me with a snarky comment in front of another employee, I'll say 'Geoff, let's take this offline. Meet with me after today's meeting.'"

When you're writing strategies, allow yourself to list them freely, without any self-censorship. Then, return to your list and pick those you'll try.

Please take two minutes and make your list.

Strategy #7: Design Your Game Plan

Designing a game plan cements your likelihood of success. Well-formulated game plans chart when you'll start each strategy and the resources you'll need to implement each one. Because you can't always start every strategy immediately, establishing dates helps you keep on track toward meeting your goal.

Resources vary widely. One of my clients took up the Korean martial art of tae kwon do to develop her self-confidence. Another client used me as a resource: He made me his sounding board as he formulated how he'd present his situation to upper management.

Strategy #8: Set Mileposts and Establish a Follow-up Method

Setting mileposts helps you stay on top of your progress. A milepost defines exactly what you hope to happen by specific intermediary dates as you head toward goal attainment.

Specific mileposts also remind you that you're making progress even if you experience minor setbacks. For example, someone who hopes to lose twenty-one pounds may set a milepost for losing four pounds a month. Then, even if she hits a plateau or regains a pound or two during a week, she can see that by the end of each month she has consistently lost four pounds. If you establish a goal relating to self-confidence, you may become disheartened if you backed down from a challenge. By setting mileposts, you can remind yourself of the progress you're making.

You'll also want to establish a method for keeping your goal "front and center" in your mind. One of my clients placed his game plan on his home computer in the "quick launch at start-up" and saw it each time he powered on his computer. Another printed her game plan and posted it next to her bedroom mirror.

Following is a model game plan worksheet. In the sample that follows, I've entered possible strategies, start times, resources, and mileposts for the hypothetical goal of responding to snarky comments. I recommend that you create one just like it on paper or on your computer to set a weekly milepost for what you want to see achieved for each strategy you plan to use to achieve your goal or goals.

MY GAME PLAN

Goal: ____

STRATEGIES	WHEN I'LL START	RESOURCES NEEDED	MILEPOST

SAMPLE GAME PLAN

Goal: *Respond assertively to snarky statements.*

STRATEGIES	WHEN I'LL START	RESOURCES NEEDED	MILEPOST
Develop and practice a list of professional yet "stop the put-down" statements	Tonight	My brain and an hour tonight and practice sessions in two nights	I'll have a list of five to ten statements by the weekend
Learn to breathe so I can think straight if I'm caught off-guard	Right now	Twelve minutes to practice breathing tonight and a way to cue myself that I need to breathe	Does it work tomorrow at work when I'm confronted? Does it work the next time I'm in a staff meeting and confronted?

Strategy #9: Start Now

Your final strategy: Do something *right now* that gets you working toward one of your goals. Develop a plan; make notes on your desk or computer calendar about the action steps you'll accomplish on certain days. Or just simply . . . *start.*

Congratulations. You're on your way.

Your Turn: Where Are You Now?

1. If you've set a goal, reflect on how it felt to create one. If you haven't yet established a goal, what stands in your way? Imagine I'm sitting in front of you and asking you what you want to change. What did you answer? Whatever your first thought was, that's your goal.
2. If you haven't yet done so, fill out your game plan worksheet.
3. What's the most helpful idea or strategy you gained from working through these goal-setting and game-planning exercises?
4. How do you feel about the time frames and mileposts you've created in your game plan?
5. What might stop you from carrying out your game plan? Are there any barriers or obstacles that might get in your way? How do you plan to tackle each of them?
6. When you set goals in the past, perhaps a New Year's resolution, was there something that led you to give up or decide to retreat into your comfort zone? What was it? How will you recognize it next time and how will you handle it differently?

THE RIGHT WAY TO ASK MANAGERS AND OTHERS FOR WHAT YOU NEED

Valor grows by daring, fear by holding back.

—PUBLILIUS SYRUS

When **TOM'S BOSS ASKED** him why he'd omitted Caren's part of the team report, he'd replied, "I wasn't able to get it from her." To his shock and dismay, his boss told him Caren had already given her a draft and scolded, "Next time, ask her for her ideas."

Tom opened his mouth, and then shut it, not knowing what to say. Caren, a shape-shifter, had thrown him under the bus—and she wasn't even in the room. He remembered Caren's response when he asked her for it. First she said, "I didn't know I was supposed to write anything," and when pressed by him, she matter-of-factly said, "I don't have time," and turned away from him.

Tom wanted to ask his boss for her help in handling Caren, but knew his boss considered her a model employee and would blame him for the fractured coworker relationship. Like other shape-shifter employees, Caren knew how to kiss up and kick down laterally.

FOUR FACTORS TO FOCUS ON WHEN ENLISTING SUPPORT

Do you need to convince a senior manager to rein in a workplace bully? Do you want to gain a coworker's support in facing off against a bully or in presenting a case to a senior manager? Before you approach anyone—boss or coworker—for help, consider these four key factors and the part they'll play in gaining agreement.

1. Tap the Emotional Component to Buy-in

Think of a purchase you've made in the last several years that was more expensive than you'd planned. Write or mentally list the reasons why you almost didn't buy it. Was it the cost, doubts about whether you needed it, concern that it might not do what the salesperson said it would do, or . . . ?

Next, write or think about the reasons that propelled you to buy it. Was it simply that you wanted it, felt you deserved it, knew you'd love how it made you feel, or . . . ?

Now, review the two lists. If you're like most people, the reasons you made the purchase are more emotional than logical, and the reasons you almost didn't purchase the item are more logical than emotional. If you want someone to buy what you're selling or to buy into what you're asking, realize that just as emotions rule in making purchasing decisions so do they in buying into another's ideas.

To increase the emotional likelihood that someone will agree to what you ask, you have to understand why people want to do things.

First, people do things for those they like and trust. They listen to those they can relate to, who seem to understand their perspective, and who they feel present information honestly. If you attack or blame another person when you're making a request for support, you're likely to turn the person off.

Second, those you ask for something want to feel their own needs will be met. We all listen to the same radio station, WIFM or "what's in it for me?" Before you ask anyone for assistance, think about who they are and what they care about. Is it, for example, doing the right thing, their own or their department's productivity, protecting themselves, maintaining their employees' morale, or . . . ?

2. Make the Bully—Not You—the Problem

When you lay a problem in another person's lap, she may see you as the problem, which can lead her to "shoot the messenger." If you're asking management to rein in a bully and want to be seen as presenting, not creating, a problem, demonstrate the ways in which the bully poses a problem to managers and the organization.

If you can prove the bully is a legal liability to senior managers, you can motivate them to act. For example, if a bully attacks you because of your race or sex, as Mike attacked Cynthia, you can get management's attention. Unless you work in a state like California, in which bullying is illegal, you need to realize that terms like *hostile environment* may mean one thing to you—this bully makes working here miserable—but something completely different in a legally, actionable sense.

Because bullying isn't illegal in most states, and if your organization lacks an anti-bullying policy, you'll need to clearly outline the other costs the bully creates. Have many employees left because of the bully? What other risks and liabilities does the organization take on due to the bully's treatment of you and others? If you present the situation correctly to an individual concerned about these risks, you have a chance to topple the bully from his throne.

When you present this information, present it factually and calmly. You want your manager to feel that you're educating, not blaming, her, and also that you're not complaining.

3. Provide Effective Documentation

If you want someone to act after you've presented a problem, you need to provide something more substantial than your opinion or anecdotal information. Documentation is crucial to obtaining buy-in. Effective documentation presents hard facts that lead the person who reads them to the conclusion you want. If you simply offer your opinion, it rarely works, as the person may doubt you've reached the correct conclusion.

Your documentation should be factual, accurate, and objective, rather than subjective. Record the specific facts most likely to lead someone else to draw the same conclusions you did. If you need to present a subjective issue, describe what actually happened, without including your opinion or conclusions about it.

A call that I received from a manager who wanted to terminate a sixty-year-old woman, Tish, illustrates how important documentation is for convincing others. When the manager called me, saying he wanted to terminate Tish, I asked him why. He said that she was nasty, had a poor attitude, and made everyone around her miserable. He knew if he fired her, she'd sue, and he feared a jury would see her as a sweet, little old lady. Because this woman scared him, he'd never documented any of her problem behavior.

I went over the case with him and wrote his documentation for him. As you read it, imagine that you're a jury member; then decide what you think about this sweet, grandmotherly employee. "Tish arrived at the scheduled 1 p.m. staff meeting at 1:50 p.m.; she was apparently back late from lunch. She took a chair in the back row, moved it two feet farther away, crossed her arms, and closed her eyes. When I called on her to ask what she thought about the parking agreement the staff had just made, she rolled her eyes and said, 'How the f--- should I know?'"

Does this fact-based documentation give you a new view of Tish? Effective documentation tells the story without editorial comments but with supporting detail.

4. Learn How to Negotiate

Although you may want senior management to accept what you say and act immediately, the managers may wonder if you're simply an employee with a grudge. They have to consider the big picture also—

bullies often produce sterling results. Consequently, you need effective negotiation skills.

The best negotiators begin by determining the outcomes they want. What do you want most? Do you want upper management to investigate the situation by interviewing other employees before firing or disciplining the bully or do you hope to be moved to a position where you'll be immune from further bullying? Always establish your ideal objectives, as negotiators tend to achieve results in proportion to their expectations.

In addition to deciding what you want most, determine your bottom line. You don't need to tell senior management what this is, but you'll feel more grounded in your negotiation if you've decided the minimum result you feel comfortable with and what you'll do if you don't get it. This becomes your fallback position. For example, if management doesn't act, will you simply ask for a well-worded letter of reference to enable you to seek a new position in another organization?

Knowledge is power in negotiations. Prior to meeting with any senior manager, learn as much as you can about the manager and his or her perspective. LinkedIn and other social media sites make this relatively easy. For example, you may learn that your manager frequents the *Harvard Business Review* forum on LinkedIn. If so, this manager might respond to a thoughtfully presented argument, backed up by research. Who evaluates this senior manager and on what basis? What matters more to this manager—high productivity or low employee turnover? How does the manager benefit from tackling this bully?

Ahead of the meeting, try to anticipate the objections a manager may have to taking action based on what you present. You can then include your counterargument when you meet—for example, "You may be wondering whether my suggestion that you interview all employees to learn what's really going on will create a furor. I can assure you that other employees with whom I've spoken will greet this survey with relief."

If, instead of a senior manager, you're planning to meet with a coworker in the hope that you can get him to join forces with you, what objections do you anticipate? How will you address them in a way that doesn't put your coworker on the defensive? Prepare in advance what you might say to calm his fears.

Whenever you meet with a senior manager, begin with a statement that establishes a positive context for the meeting. You might start by saying, "I've very much enjoyed my five years working here and feel great loyalty to the organization. I know also that you value both employee morale and productivity." Never present your ideas for change in a way that seems motivated by self-interest. When you couch what you say in terms of how it impacts the manager and the organization, you make it more appealing.

Although you might be tempted to talk nonstop during your meeting with the senior manager, rein yourself in. Monologues convince no one and often lead the person you're trying to convince to tune you out.

Instead, intersperse questions with the facts. After all, what will a senior manager believe more readily, what the manager says in response to your questions, or what you say? By asking questions, you also learn how the manager views what you're saying.

When you ask questions, two words to avoid are *why* and *did.* Both lead to defensiveness. If you hoped a senior manager would have acted sooner, perhaps when the bully ran off the last person in that position, and you ask "What led you not to act?" you create a different feeling than if you ask "Why haven't you acted?" Regardless of your words, keep your energy positive and nonjudgmental as you ask the question so your manager doesn't feel put on the spot.

If you thought this senior manager should have realized how beaten down you and other employees were by your bully supervisor when the manager sat in on a recent staff meeting, you might ask, "What was your sense of what happened at the staff meeting you attended?" This open-ended question will give you a different response than if you ask, "Did you see what he did and how other employees reacted?" Never imply criticism with your questions.

Questions such as "What leads you to see it that way?" or "Please help me understand your reasoning" draw out your manager, allowing you to learn the hidden objections you need to counter if your manager is going to act as you hope.

Finally, you may want to ask your manager to keep the fact that you sought assistance confidential or to offer you an assurance against retaliation.

Your Turn: Where Are You Now?

You may not want to ask someone for support at this moment, but have you ever wanted to ask for someone's support? Did you? Answer the following questions based on that experience. If your answer to the question is "No," imagine what it might be like if you did and answer the questions accordingly.

1. Who do you want to convince or whose support do you need to enlist? What matters to this individual? What might lead this person to want to help you?
2. If you plan to meet with a senior manager, you should outline the risks or liabilities the bully creates.
3. Take a day to write or collect documentation. Before you give it to anyone, make sure it's factual, specific, and objective. Then, review it. If you weren't personally involved in the situation, would it convince you to act?
4. Select a senior manager or HR representative to whom you'll be presenting the information. Do an Internet search and learn more about him or her.
5. Prepare for negotiation. What outcome do you hope to achieve? What's your bottom line; what will you do if you don't achieve what you hope?

6. What objections do you anticipate? How do you plan to counter them?
7. Before you meet with a senior manager, create your opening statement. What will you say that starts the meeting on a positive note?
8. In the next week, eliminate the words *why* and *did* from your vocabulary. Instead, start any questions you ask with "What," "How," or "Can you tell me more."
9. Ask a friend to role-play a senior manager. Provide your friend with objections you anticipate and ask your friend to make the meeting "hard on you." By practicing the meeting ahead of time, you'll handle it better in real life.

ANGER, THE BULLY, AND YOU

How few there are who have courage enough to own their faults, or resolution enough to mend them.

—BENJAMIN FRANKLIN

WHEN CASSANDRA LEARNED the depth and breadth of what character assassin Heather had told others about her, she said she felt "so mad I could spit nails." She called me for a coaching session and vented with almost volcanic rage. "Let's take a walk so you can talk it out," I suggested. We headed to Anchorage's Coastal Trail. Initially Cassandra yelled so loudly that birds flew from nearby trees and passing dogs and their owners moved off the trail as they neared us.

To handle the bully in your work life, you may need to learn to handle anger—the bully's and yours. Bullies intimidate others through anger and other types of overt aggression. When you finally decide to stand up to a bully, you may lift the lid off a vat of buried emotions and learn how angry you are—at both the bully and yourself for taking the mistreatment for so long.

Anger differs from danger by only one letter.

HOW TO HANDLE A BULLY'S ANGER

Bullies use anger to intimidate. They off-load their stress by blowing up at others. Bullies even justify this by saying, "I only got mad because you didn't do what I told you to do" or "I yelled because you didn't listen."

A bully's anger may set off your fight-or-flight response. Never fight aggression with aggression; it only throws gasoline on the fire. Instead of counterattacking, use coastline breathing to calm yourself and stop you from reacting precipitously. Arguing may make you feel better in the short term, but it can lead to retaliation in the long run.

Although you may want to exit a situation for your own safety or to de-escalate a confrontation, retreat generally provides only a short-term solution. Bullies often fixate on and come after targets. If you've been on the run from a bully in your work life, you may need to enlist the help of human resources or a senior manager, or learn to stand firm.

Finally, never take a bully's anger personally. It's truly the bully's problem, not yours.

HOW TO MANAGE YOUR OWN ANGER

Targets often discover, to their chagrin, that they're angry—at the bully, at their organizations for placing them in harm's way, and at themselves for allowing a bully to trample on them.

When you smother anger and the accompanying resentment under an "I'm not really bothered" facade, these negative emotions turn inward and fester. Dwelling on how you've been bullied may increase your anger. When you let yourself realize how truly angry you are, you may be tempted to react impulsively.

Rein yourself in and translate your anger into action. Ask yourself: What will fix the situation? What underlying issues need to be addressed? It may help to talk the situation through with a trusted adviser who can help you design constructive strategies or a game plan you can implement.

Just as a pressure cooker has a safety valve, you may need someone to whom you can express the depth of your anger, so it doesn't trip you up at work. Cassandra later told me that having a safe time and place to vent allowed her to calmly give her convention speech later that day.

It's important to remember that refusing to show your anger doesn't mean you let the bully off the hook. As the saying goes, "Don't get mad, get even."

ARE YOU A BULLY? (IF SO, HOW TO NOT BE ONE)

While reading earlier chapters, you may have wondered if you are a bully. You may be. Here's the good news: If you wonder if you're a bully, you've likely started on the road to not being one. Bullies are made and can unmake themselves.

What Makes a Bully?

You may have become or act like a bully because you:

- ☐ Learned how to bully from a parent
- ☐ Need to win or don't have other ways to get what you want
- ☐ Feel justified in how you treat others
- ☐ Are compensating for feeling less worthy than others
- ☐ Are distracting yourself from examining the areas in yourself that you need to fix by bullying others

Where It All Began: What Made Them Bullies

Three real-life stories may help you look at yourself and how you learned—and may be able to unlearn—your bullying patterns. You may also realize that bullies, while aggressors, may be victims themselves, of their own history, delusional rationalizations, and problematic relationships resulting from their bullish behavior. Once you identify what made you a bully, you can decide whether or not to remain one.

Andy, who bullied Suzanne, was raised by a weak parent who gave in to his every whim. Like any other two-year-old, Andy threw temper tantrums. When he did, he got whatever he wanted. Bullying worked for Andy, and he kept it up.

When Annette refused to put up with Andy's temper tantrums and sent his stormy email to her supervisor and an HR manager, they told Andy to cut it out, as Andy's mom should have done. After that, Andy toed the line when he interacted with Annette, although he continued bullying others whenever he could get away with it.

If you're an Andy-type bully, you bully because you can get away with it, and like the reward it provides.

As a child, Stevie watched her father abuse and intimidate her mother. Although she often stepped between them to protect her mom, she loved being daddy's little girl. Because he spoke with authority, she always believed what he told her. Her parents divorced when Stevie was a preteen. Stevie idolized her father, who turned her into his surrogate wife. He made up stories about her mother and she believed them, and held her mother responsible for the divorce. As a result, Stevie bullied her mother and felt justified in doing so, and found that it helped ease her own pain. Unwittingly, Stevie had modeled herself on a bully and brought her bullying behaviors with her into the workplace, where she used them on women who got in her way.

Bullies like Stevie learn bullying from parents they identify with, who convince them bullying can be justified.

Silent grenade Mike was a self-confessed workplace bully, with no intention of changing his ways. Instead, he expected others to feel sorry for him when he told them, "My dad whipped me. I've got the scars on my back to prove it. I can't help who I am. I learned, early on, that it is survival of the fittest."

Bullies like Mike grew up to bully others as they were bullied.

And you; are you a bully? If so, what made you one? Are you as much of a prisoner of the way you treat others as your targets? Are the rewards you garner worth the quality work relationships you'll never achieve? If you want to end your bullying career, realize that all the reasons illustrated in these stories are just excuses.

Your Turn: Where Are You Now?

1. What real-life examples have you seen that involve angry bullies?
2. How has their anger and behavior affected you?
3. How has their anger and behavior affected others?
4. What did you or others do to cope? What worked? What didn't work? What did you learn?
5. What's the best advice you can give someone who faces an angry bully?
6. Who or what are you angry at?
7. What will you do differently should you encounter an angry bully?
8. What will you do differently with your own anger?
9. Do you know a bully or do you fear you're a bully? What reasons does this person have, or what reasons do you have?
10. What can you do to stop a bully?
11. What does it take to stop a bully on the part of the bully?

WHAT EVERY LEADER SHOULD KNOW ABOUT BULLYING

All that is necessary for the triumph of evil is for good men to do nothing.

—EDMUND BURKE

DANA CONSIDERED HERSELF A princess; spoiled by her parents and armed with a college degree in business management, Dana viewed herself as a prize hire. During college, she had worked part-time in her family's business, where managers and coworkers alike treated her with kid gloves. Dana decided she wanted bigger and better things and applied for a management trainee position at Lentos.

Dana's bosses were pleased with her performance during her first three months and fast-tracked her into a junior manager position. Rather than being pleased, Dana wondered why she hadn't been promoted to manager. After all, she had a degree and worked as hard as any manager.

When she dealt with those subordinate to her, Dana adopted the same imperious mannerisms she believed served her well in her parents' company, which led to multiple run-ins with support staff, including one that left a well-liked receptionist in tears when Dana flew into a rage because the receptionist routed a call to her just before 5 p.m. Dana didn't like staying after 5:00. "She's scary," the receptionist told her coworkers during lunch the next day. "She revved from 0 to 100 miles an hour, just like that!"

Soon Dana began snapping at her peers when she thought they got in her way. Although Lentos emphasized a collaborative, team culture, Dana viewed herself as a star player and expected her coworkers to recognize this and defer to her as employees at her family's business had. Her Lentos peers began referring to Dana as El Queen.

Coworkers noticed that she regularly texted personal messages on company time. When Roger showed up at her office for a meeting and found her texting, he waited politely in the doorway. When she looked up, he walked in, pointed to her cell, and teasingly asked, "Big date?"

"How dare you!" Dana yelled, her eyes bulging in outrage.

"Uh, I'm here for our meeting," said Roger.

"I don't have time!" And that was it for their meeting.

When Dana completed projects, she expected accolades. When her managers gave her both positive and constructive feedback, they soon learned Dana couldn't take criticism and rationalized any errors she'd made. In her fifth month, Dana had several run-ins with another junior manager, Stephanie. Both had brittle personalities and took offense easily. Both glowered whenever they were in each other's presence.

Lentos's senior management team asked Lanie, a kind-hearted senior manager tasked with mentoring junior managers, to mediate the problem. Lanie took Stephanie and then Dana aside. Stephanie told Lanie that Dana had made unforgiveable comments about her.

"Like what?"

"I don't remember them all," responded Stephanie, "but she yelled 'Look, b----, get out of my face' when I asked her for her department's data. I'm okay with someone blowing off steam, but she was out of control."

When Lanie took Dana aside, Dana said, "I gave her the data. She expected me to hold her hand. I don't baby others and don't expect them to baby me."

Lanie tried counseling Dana. "We hired and promoted you because we saw promise. I'm hoping you can learn from what's happened recently. In my career, I've learned you get the treatment from others that you give them. Your coworkers think you are volatile."

"That's their problem," retorted Dana.

"Is any part of your relationship with Stephanie or other employees your problem?" asked Lanie.

Dana stiffened; she angrily responded, "I don't see how, and I don't appreciate being talked to like a three-year-old."

Lanie told the management team that Dana reeked of outrage and self-righteousness during their meeting. Lentos terminated Dana and gave her a letter of recommendation that stated the company viewed her as a promising manager-in-training who would be better suited to a company with a more aggressive culture.

Shocked by her termination, Dana stormed out of the building. The next day she called, demanding a meeting with Lentos's chief executive officer. She arrived with her attorney and, with her jaw thrust out, protested that she hadn't felt supported as a new manager; that her reference letter was insulting, given all she'd done for Lentos; that she wanted a more complimentary letter or none at all; and then threatened that if she didn't get six months' severance pay, she'd sue.

"Consider the letter rescinded," responded the CEO. He then turned to Dana's attorney, saying, "Since a lawsuit's been mentioned, this meeting is concluded. Here's our attorney's phone number, along with documentation from our investigation into Dana's last thirty days with Lentos."

THREE REASONS LEADERS AVOID CONFRONTING BULLIES

Bullies rip apart an organization's culture, poison employee morale, and destroy productivity; nevertheless, leaders shy away from tackling bullies. What can leaders do if they're committed to eliminating bullying from their work environment?

Three factors protect and even immunize bullies.

Reason #1: Leaders' Blind Spot

"Leaders have a blind spot concerning bullies," notes Dr. Gary Namie, cofounder and director of the internationally known Workplace Bullying Institute. "Because bullies generally treat senior executives differently, often doing personal favors for them, leaders reflexively defend them, saying, 'That's not the Bob I know.' Leaders need to recognize that bullies ingratiate themselves with apple-polishing behaviors. Everyone else sees the con, but not the leader."

Reason #2: The Bully Exemption

Although bullies damage morale and productivity in the long run, they often produce great short-term results. This leads some senior executives to embrace the bully as a hard-charging, bottom line–oriented taskmaster, claiming, "Say what you will, he gets results." When employees or peers complain about such bullies, their concerns fall on deaf ears.

Reason #3: Fear—Are They Talking About Me, Too?

Bullies and those having a bad day demonstrate similar behaviors. A senior manager with his or her own flash temper may wonder, "If this behavior constitutes bullying, could I also be accused?" Because of the overlap between bullying and problem behaviors others demonstrate, many organizations hesitate to enact anti-bullying policies, claiming it's too hard to define bullying.

FOUR WAYS LEADERS CAN CREATE A BULLY-FREE WORK ENVIRONMENT

Because of leaders' status, no one bullies them, and the chain of command works against employees at the lower and middle levels of the organization, who are unable to voice their concerns directly to senior executives. Nevertheless, there are ways to solve this problem.

Solution #1: Don't Ignore the Warning Signs

"Leaders need to be enough in tune with employee morale to recognize the tell-tale signs that bullying is occurring in their organizations," advises Namie. When employees raise issues, Namie notes that all too often, "Leaders fail to appreciate the invaluable feedback on employee morale their employees provide. Instead, leaders give bullies impunity, responding, 'That's just Bob,'" leaving employees to realize they need to put up with the bully and shut up.

One of the best tools for obtaining employee feedback is the 360° review, discussed in earlier chapters, which allows employees and peers to confidentially answer questions that ask how managers, supervisors, and others treat them.

Solution #2: Create a Bully-Free Work Environment

Leaders set the tone for their organizations. If you're a leader who cares, ask yourself these four questions:

1. Do you model respect toward all employees?
2. Do you listen to and address voiced concerns?
3. Do you let all staff know what is and is not acceptable behavior?
4. Do you encourage open, confidential reporting?

If you haven't answered "Yes" to all four questions, begin changing what you're doing now.

Solution #3: Establish an Anti-Bullying Policy

A well-written anti-bullying policy can help leaders purge unrepentant bullies.

Model Anti-Bullying Policy

Former attorney turned HR consultant Richard Birdsall and I co-authored the following sample policy, which you may use:

Workplace bullying and harassment can inflict serious harm upon targeted employees. All employees have the right to be treated with dignity and respect at work.

Accordingly, it is a violation of (Company) policy to engage in abusive conduct. No form of harassment will be permitted or condoned.

Abusive conduct includes acts and/or omissions that a reasonable person would find abusive, based on the severity, nature, and frequency of the conduct, including but not limited to:

- Repeated verbal abuse such as the use of derogatory remarks, insults, and epithets;
- Verbal, nonverbal, or physical conduct of a threatening, intimidating, or humiliating nature;
- The sabotage or undermining of an employee's work performance or opportunity for promotion or advancement.

Employees are encouraged to report bullying behavior without fear of retaliation. Employees may report harassment and abusive conduct to any senior manager or member of the Human Resources team.

Employees engaged in harassment or abusive conduct, or those who retaliate against an individual for reporting such alleged behavior, may be subject to disciplinary action up to and including termination.

Solution #4: Create a Viable Grievance Channel

Fear and the habit of silence allow many bullies to skate under the radar. When individuals do come forward, they often face increased retaliatory bullying. Leaders need to create a viable grievance channel that provides targets with confidentiality and assurance that their concerns will be addressed. In the model anti-bullying policy, targets may go to any member of senior management or Human Resources, which allows them to skirt the chain of command if necessary.

Your Turn: Where Are You Now?

If you are not in a leadership position, imagine what it would be like to be in one, and answer the following questions accordingly.

1. Have you seen evidence of the bully blind spot among your managers, or in yourself? What didn't you or the manager see or hear?
2. Have you experienced the bully exemption where a bully was allowed to "get away with murder" because of the results the bully or the work group under the bully produced? What was the effect? What did management need to realize about the cost of that bully exemption?
3. What distinguishes a bully from another individual who exhibits problem behaviors?
4. If you're a leader, how do you plan to get "in tune" with staff at lower levels to learn what's going on from their perspective?
5. What benefits would the model anti-bullying policy provide your organization? If you like it, arrange a visit with a senior executive or human resources professional in your organization and offer it to them, free of charge.
6. Does your organization have a viable grievance channel? If not, what do you propose to do about it?

WHAT HUMAN RESOURCES CAN AND SHOULD DO

People always say I didn't give up my seat because I was tired, but that isn't true. . . . No, the only tired I was, was tired of giving in.

—ROSA PARKS

WHEN HR MANAGER JESS heard supervisor Ray's voice on the phone, her heart sank. Ray, a Darth Vader clone, ran through employees like water. Some he fired; others got so fed up they quit. So when he told Jess, "I need you to fire Rose," she groaned. What now?

"Ray, what's the problem?"

"Ever since Rose was diagnosed with breast cancer, she's been in and out of the office for doctors' appointments."

"Ray, it's understandable that she's missed some work. She has cancer."

Steam in his voice, Ray barked his response. "Maybe you HR types think that's okay but everyone in my department needs to produce. I can't keep someone who can't work the hours it takes to meet deadlines. Rose claims she needs to leave by 5:00, and that's not how it works in accounting."

"What a jerk," thought Jess, tamping down her irritation. "We went over this last month. The Americans with Disabilities Act requires us to accommodate employees with disabilities. Cancer qualifies."

"Stupid law. Move her to another department. I expect you to take care of this." Ray delivered this line like an order.

"Not a bad idea," thought Jess. "Rose deserves to get away from Ray, but move her to which department?" Jess knew Rose needed her job for medical insurance and viewed her work in accounting as a rock on which she could depend.

"I will take care of it," thought Jess, "but probably not the way Mr. Empathy wants."

"Ray, do you want to come to my office or should I visit you?" she asked.

"I don't have a lot of time."

"I'll come to you."

"So, Ray, what's got you amped up?"

Ray snorted and spoke through thin lips, "An endless series of medical appointments, more frequently now that she's got radiation every day."

"For how long?"

"That's not the point."

"And the point is?"

"I need a full-time employee."

"You have one. Rose has been and is a great employee. She has cancer. We need to accommodate her."

"She was a decent employee. She's not anymore. Put her somewhere else."

"I'll look into that. Meanwhile, I expect you to treat her appropriately. And we're going to talk about what that means."

Ray shot up from his chair. "I don't have time for this."

Jess stood and eyed him. "Fine, you choose. Ten minutes with me now, or two hours of discrimination, anti-harassment, and retaliation training later." Ray stormed out.

"Two hours it would be," thought Jess, knowing Ray would try to get out of the training by saying he'd already taken it. It clearly hadn't sunk in. Ray needed to learn that the law was on Rose's side. Jess planned to meet with Rose to reassure her, write up a short memo on the turnover rate in Ray's department, advise the CEO, Paul, and provide Ray's training herself.

The next morning, at the close of the monthly managers' meeting, Paul said, "Jess and Ray, could you two stay a few minutes?"

"So what's up with you two?" Paul asked.

Ray shot Jess a pointed look. "As I told you, Paul, our hotshot HR guru isn't letting me run my department."

Realizing Ray had already briefed Paul on his side of the story, Jess knew she needed to think, not skirmish.

"Ms. HR has time to sit in her office singing 'Kumbaya.' I'm trying to keep our company fiscally on track, and I can't do that unless accounting is fully staffed."

"Ray, your department is fully staffed."

"Her friend, Rose, has a medical appointment every day," Ray continued, as if Jess hadn't spoken, "and refuses to work overtime, forcing others to carry her load."

"Paul, I checked into this. I want to remind you both that the three of us know Rose's medical issues on a limited need-to-know basis. That said, Rose needs a five-minute radiation treatment daily for six weeks. Paul, she schedules this so she's their first appointment when they open at 8:00 in the morning and gets to the office by 8:30, which is another demonstration of her work ethic. She's finishing the second of six weeks of treatment. She has lunch at her desk to accommodate the thirty-minute morning delay, so it's hardly a crisis."

Ray ignored what Jess said, continuing like the drill sergeant he was. "I expect everyone in my department to be at work by 8:00 and work until 5:00 or 6:00 at a minimum. Rose refuses to schedule these appointments after work or to work past 5:00."

"I checked into that as well. The radiation oncology department schedules appointments between 8:00 and 4:00 and they don't schedule appointments at lunchtime. We need to accommodate Rose or any other employee who has a disability. Expecting more than full-time work isn't accommodation."

Ray's lips tightened. "Accounting has deadlines."

"So does HR, but let's get to the real problem here," Jess said. "She has cancer, Paul, and both federal and state laws require us to accommodate any employee with a disability. What's more, this goes beyond legal issues. Rose has earned our loyalty with five years of solid performance."

REAL-WORLD TACTICS THAT WORK

As Jess demonstrated, effective human resources professionals erect a bulwark against Darth Vader clone supervisors and other bullies.

Strategy #1: Make a Business Case

By making a business case, HR can convince the organization's leaders to stop paying the bottom-line costs for bullying. Bullies demoralize employees, reducing employee productivity. Abusive work environments have other serious consequences for employers, including higher turnover and absenteeism rates and increases in medical and workers' compensation claims.

In Rose's case, Jess was able to point out to the CEO and the supervisor that federal and state law protected the employee. Jess also reminded the CEO of the ethical reasons for supporting a long-term employee.

Strategy #2: Create an Anti-Bullying Policy

Such a policy can be standalone or can be added to the company's current harassment policy. It could, for example, say that harassment of any individual, not just those in protected classes, will not be tolerated. There's a sample policy in Chapter 25. The Society for Human Resource Management's 2011 survey reports that 56 percent of all companies have an anti-bullying policy.

Strategy #3: Intervene Directly and Provide Training

HR can intervene directly with bully managers, supervisors, and employees. It can also provide managers and supervisors with the training they need to make certain that they understand their role in preventing and addressing bullying. Without training, some managers and supervisors view allegations of bullying as a messy hot potato they prefer to dodge.

Strategy #4: Train Employees

By providing employees at all levels with the skills they need to handle verbal confrontation, conflict, and bullies, they will not only learn how to deal with the situation, they will know that management stands behind them.

Strategy #5: Provide an Effective Grievance Channel for Reporting Bullying

With this mechanism, HR professionals can listen to targets and witnesses who voice concerns about bullies, keep what is said as confidential as possible, evaluate the evidence presented, and act on what they've heard to provide targets with solutions or at least options. When provided credible evidence, HR can investigate allegations and recommend discipline, improvement-oriented coaching, or termination for bullies. HR can ensure that targets aren't met with disbelief, blame, or responses such as "What do you expect from a Type A like him?" or "That's just Darth."

Strategy #6: Audit the Organization's Internal Culture

In this way, HR can assess whether the organization promotes respect and dignity. HR can sponsor regular employee surveys to uncover hot spots and trouble zones.

Strategy #7: Arrange 360° Reviews

Periodic reviews of managers, supervisors, and other professionals provide those interacting with bullying managers, supervisors, or peers the opportunity to provide confidential feedback concerning problem behavior. In 360° reviews, seven to eleven individuals who interact with the review subject respond to questions such as "What can you say about how this manager works with employees and peers?" "How does this manager handle leadership?" "What can you say about how this manager communicates, and handles those with a different viewpoint?" and "Is this manager fair and reasonable?" If bullying exists, a well-done 360° review generally uncovers it.

Strategy #8: Provide Mediation

HR professionals can act as intermediaries between alleged bullies and their targets to create agreements for future communication and interaction. If the bully violates the mediation agreement, it makes disciplining or terminating the bully easier.

Strategy #9: Remove Bullies from the Organization

Although this is difficult and time-consuming, if presented with credible evidence, HR can make the case to fire the bully.

Your Turn: Where Are You Now?

1. What did the HR manager, Jess, do well?
2. What traps did Jess avoid?
3. Was there a trap she fell into?
4. How did Jess handle Ray's snide comments?
5. What other tactics did Ray use?
6. What could Jess have done even better?
7. Whether you're an HR professional or not, write a business

case to convince your senior management that bullying needs to be addressed.

8. If you're in HR or senior management, institute an anti-bullying policy or add language to your current harassment policy that states that any harassment of any individual, not just those in protected classes, will not be tolerated.
9. If you're in HR, design a program for providing managers and supervisors with training concerning their role in preventing and addressing bullying. If you're not in HR, petition for such a program.
10. If you're in HR, arrange training for all employees on handling verbal confrontation and workplace bullies. If you're not in HR, petition for this training.
11. If you're in HR, create an effective grievance channel for targets and witnesses.
12. If you're in HR or senior management, arrange an audit of your organization's internal culture and assess whether your organization promotes dignity and respect.
13. If you suspect a bully exists in your organization, arrange or petition for a 360° review to uncover credible evidence.

BULLYING ISN'T ILLEGAL—OR IS IT?

The significant problems we face cannot be solved at the same level of thinking with which they were created.

—ALBERT EINSTEIN

WHEN ACCOUNTING DEPARTMENT SUPERVISOR Ray complained to the CEO that accommodating an employee with cancer left his department short staffed, HR manager Jess knew she had a fight on her hands. Ray had a practice of toeing the legal line yet making an employee's life so miserable, he or she quit. Jess thought Ray was a bully, but he didn't act out in front of the CEO, and his department produced great results.

Also, although Jess reminded CEO Paul that federal and state law required their company to accommodate a disabled employee, she knew that Paul cared more about Ray's good results than he did about employees. She'd tried to fix the situation, but Ray had complained about her, and they'd both wound up being "talked to" by Paul.

After the skirmish, as she and Ray stood up to leave, Paul said, "Jess, can you hang around for a moment?"

"Sure." She watched Ray leave.

"How come this escalated to my level?"

"Ray thinks he can ignore the law and Rose's years of good work, and pressure her into working longer hours or me into finding her a position in another department." Paul's eyes narrowed. Yep, Jess thought, to save Rose's job, I have to figure out a way to get Paul to realize that quality employees deserved company loyalty and that Ray's results come at an expense.

"Jess, I expect you to keep our company in legal compliance. But we all depend on the accounting department being fully staffed. And you, as HR, are support to that department. Understood?"

Jess left, knowing the Americans with Disabilities Act's protection for Rose might not shield her from Ray's bullying.

According to mainstream thought, bullies have virtual immunity because no laws, other than the California's Workplace Violence Safety Act, specifically outlaw bullying. Bully arrogance, however, leads many bullies to step over the line into actions that are illegal. When they do, targets can take them to court and ask judges, regulatory agencies, or juries to take action against the bully.

OVER-THE-LINE BEHAVIOR: ILLEGAL DISCRIMINATION

ALTHOUGH MIKE ATTACKED every employee, when he yelled "You get your big, fat, black ass back to your desk," at Cynthia, he picked on the wrong woman. Cynthia filed a formal complaint with the Human Rights Commission, identified witnesses to Mike's verbal attack, reported that Mike had screamed the words "black ass" at her twice, and noted that no other African American employees worked for Mike. Making matters worse, he fired Cynthia, calling her an "entitled b----," handing her the ability to add unfair termination and retaliation to her original complaint.

Unaccustomed to being challenged and convinced of his dominance, Mike forgot that while he ruled within his organization, he didn't rule outside regulatory agencies. When the human rights investigator called, Mike blasted him, insisting he could call Cynthia or any other employee anything he wanted.

As Cynthia demonstrated, a bully who attacks someone protected by discrimination statutes—federal, state, or municipal—can unleash the power of the state or municipal Human Rights Commission or Equal Rights Commission or the federal Equal Employment Opportunity Commission against the bully. The federally protected categories include sex, race, color, religion, national origin, age for those forty and older, pregnancy, and disability. State statutes, municipal ordinances, and key federal executive orders often create other protected classes, such as sexual orientation.

OVER-THE-LINE BEHAVIOR: ATTACKING AN EMPLOYEE FOR EXERCISING A PROTECTED RIGHT

The Department of Labor (DOL) enforces more than 180 federal laws that protect employee rights. Bullies who unfairly retaliate against an employee who voices concerns related to these employee rights may find themselves trumped by a federal or state regulatory agency. These rights include the right to organize and to bargain collectively, to receive overtime pay if a nonexempt employee, to safety and health protection in the work environment and to related workers' compensation, and the right to privacy of personal information.

For example, the Fair Labor Standards Act protects employees from bully bosses who unfairly order employees to work overtime without allowing them to record their extra hours on their time cards. An employee can take notes that document overtime, such as time-stamped emails made shortly after arrival and just before departure or altered time cards, to the Department of Labor if he was fired for attempting to log overtime hours. Over a period of time, he may be able to demonstrate a bully supervisor's pattern of coercing employees not to claim overtime. In a DOL investigation, other employees' emails will show evidence of more than eight hours of work, even if their time cards show only eight-hour days.

The Occupational Safety and Health Act, administered by the Occupational Safety and Health Administration (OSHA), protects an employee's right to voice concerns over unsafe working conditions. The act assigns employers a "general duty" to provide employees with a workplace free from recognized, serious safety hazards. Unfortunately, this "general duty" clause applies only to conditions causing or likely to cause death or serious physical harm and does not apply to psychological or emotional harm or emotional upsets or anxiety.

An employee who protests "that [something] isn't safe" and then is told "if you won't do it, I'll find someone who will" can document the incident. In an OSHA investigation, other employees' testimony generally confirms that employees learn that they need to cross the line from safe to dangerous to keep their jobs. For example, the bully foreman in a construction company told several laborers, "We need to move fast. You don't need those safety belts." When one worker fell, it led to a safety investigation. When she blew the whistle, OSHA interviewed all laborers and found the pattern.

The National Labor Relations Act (NLRA) protects an employee's right to engage in concerted activity; that is, two or more employees may act together for their mutual aid or protection concerning the terms or conditions of their employment. When a company fired an employee for describing his supervisor as a racist in Facebook postings to a coworker Facebook friend, the employee protested that the NLRA protected his right to protest illegal discrimination. The state's Human Rights Commission agreed, investigated, and found a pattern of illegal discrimination on the part of a bully supervisor. Although bullying wasn't illegal in that state, discrimination was.

OVER-THE-LINE BEHAVIOR: RETALIATING AGAINST AN EMPLOYEE FOR EXERCISING A LEGAL RIGHT

Bullies expose themselves when they punish employees for exercising their rights. If your bully demotes you or takes away benefits or perks, and you can prove he is punishing you for protecting your legal rights, you can sue. Fifty-seven percent of all plaintiffs win retaliation lawsuits.

A Microsoft salesperson, in 2014, received an award of $2 million when Judge Tim Sulak affirmed a jury's 12 to 0 decision that key Microsoft managers and supervisors had created a hostile environment for the salesperson by undermining his work, making false accusations against him, blocking him from promotions, and otherwise marginalizing him (*Michael Mercieca, Plaintiff v. Tracey Rummel, and Microsoft Corporation, Defendants*). Sulak found the tech giant guilty of "acting with malice and reckless indifference," despite Microsoft's full-court press.

In 2012, a victimized employee fired after he reported abusive behavior by his boss (*Absey v. Echosphere LLC, Dish Network Services LLC and Marshall Hood*) won $270,000 from a Minnesota jury. Absey proved that Hood verbally and physically abused him. The court ruled that Dish didn't listen to Absey's complaints and failed to protect employees from Hood's violent outbursts.

OVER-THE-LINE BEHAVIOR: CRIMINAL ASSAULT

According to Kamer Zucker Abbott partner and attorney Eddie Keller, 2015 Lawyer of the Year in the field of Litigation, Labor and Employment for Las Vegas, "If bullying involves physical violence or threats of violence, there can be both criminal and civil causes of action for assault and battery. Other bullying tactics, such as following someone around outside the workplace, making unwelcome telephone calls, or texting and sending emails to an unwilling recipient, can violate a state's laws against stalking and cyberstalking."

The decision in *Raess v. Doescher*, a landmark workplace bullying case, supported this view. In that case, Raess, a cardiovascular surgeon, was accused of aggressively charging at Doescher, a technician, and backing him against a wall. The jury found in favor of Doescher on his assault claim and awarded him $325,000; the verdict was ultimately upheld on appeal to the Indiana Supreme Court.

OVER-THE-LINE BEHAVIOR: INTENTIONAL INFLICTION OF EMOTIONAL DISTRESS

Targets can sue bullies for abusive treatment. While these lawsuits are difficult to win, the employer may also be liable for the bully's intentional acts if it knows of the bad acts and takes no action to discipline the bully.

OVER-THE-LINE BEHAVIOR: VIOLATION OF THE COVENANT OF GOOD FAITH AND FAIR DEALING

According to general practice attorney Russell Nogg, past adjunct professor of Business Law at the University of Alaska, a skilled attorney may be able to argue that employers who have evidence of bullying and do not address it may violate the covenant of good faith and fair dealing upheld by many state courts, among them Alabama, Alaska, Arizona, California, Delaware, Idaho, Massachusetts, Montana, Nebraska, Utah, and Wyoming.

HR consultant Richard Birdsall, former special investigator for the California Department of Justice, believes that Nogg has a viable argument. "Employers have a duty to protect employees. If they fail to control the workplace, they potentially breach their duty, leading to a possible negligence claim. It is well recognized that employers who 'knew or should have known' illegal sexual harassment is occurring or occurred take on vicarious liability for failing to address the issue. A bully victim's attorney might argue this same vicarious liability extends to bullying."

When Continental pilot Tammy Blakey sued alleging other Continental pilots disparaged her, Blakey won her suit (*Blakey v. Continental Airlines*). The court ruled employers "have a duty to take effective measures to stop co-employee harassment when the employer knows or has reason to know" the harassment is "part of a pattern of harassment" in a setting "related to the workplace."

OVER-THE-LINE BEHAVIOR: VIOLATION OF PUBLIC POLICY

Nogg suggests that bullying may be found to violate public policy in the same manner as sexual harassment and race discrimination. "The concept of grossly disparate bargaining power has been a basis for various provisions of some contracts as void and thus against public policy. Aggrieved employees may not have reasonable bargaining power and thus can't create on their own a bully-free work environment."

OVER-THE- LINE BEHAVIOR: VIOLATION OF STATE LAW

In 2014, Tennessee passed a bill outlawing workplace bullying in its public agencies. The law requires a state body to create a training program against workplace bullying.

As of January 1, 2015, legislation requires employers in California with fifty or more workers to include anti–workplace bullying training every two years along with sexual harassment training.

On March 23, 2015, Utah became the fourteenth state to introduce the Health Workplace Bill, which has been signed off on by the Utah Senate and House. This bill compels the State Personnel Department to provide annual employee training concerning abusive conduct.

These three state bills signal a turning of the tide; you can expect more anti-bullying legislation in the future.

Your Turn: Where Are You Now?

1. Based on what you've read, is it possible you have legal rights a bully may have violated? Which ones? What do you intend to do about it? Your state's bar association can give you a list of employment attorneys to contact.
2. Does your state have anti-bullying legislation? If not, consider writing your legislators and asking them to sponsor a bill.

THE TIMES ARE CHANGING: HAVE YOU?

Life shrinks or expands in proportion
to one's courage.

—ANAÏS NIN

"CONNIE, WE'RE WAITING ON you at the bike trail."

"Abby, I can't make it."

"You're working late again?"

"Yeah."

"You have to stand up for yourself," Abby said in a firm voice.

"I know."

"So did you tell him you won't work past 6:00?"

"No," answered Connie in a small voice.

"Why the heck not?" asked Abby, her voice rising.

"I wanted to, but . . . ," Connie's voice trailed off. "He looked so mad when he told me I had to get this done before I left."

"He's just a bully. You said you'd stand firm."

"I know."

"So why do you let people walk all over you?"

Familiar story?

All of us have patterns for handling conflict, which directly affect how we handle bullies.

Some of us are pushovers; we learned this early in life. We signal our intimidation to bullies and they sense, correctly, that they can walk on us without negative consequences.

Others of us learn to go toe-to-toe with those who mess with us, and the bullies leave us alone or decide we're exactly who they want to fight to prove they're the toughest dog in the ring.

The inventory below gives you an opportunity to learn your preferred conflict style. Once you identify your own style, in contrast with other approaches, you can add new approaches that appeal to you to your repertoire.

DISCOVER YOUR CONFLICT STYLE AND THE APPROACH THAT'S RIGHT FOR YOU

As you take this inventory, honesty counts. Don't answer as you think you "should," answer as you "are." Select the alternative(s) that fits how you truly act (even if you know you should do things differently).

Read each situation and consider the six alternatives. Then, divide ten points among the choices according to which alternative(s) best describes you. For example, in the first question, if you really like answer "C," give "C" ten points and the other alternatives zero. If, however, you like answer "C" but also like "A" and "B," split the ten points, giving the most points to the alternative you like the best and so on down the line.

Curry Conflict Inventory

You glance at the phone number listed on the incoming call. You recognize the phone number of someone with whom you don't want to interact. You:

Don't answer. A____

Take the call. What the heck? You might as well handle the situation now. B____

Immediately think about how you can work things out, and pick up the phone, hoping to ask questions, not tick the caller off, and work out a resolution.	C_____
Take the phone call because you don't want to make the caller angrier and aren't sure there's a better option.	D_____
Take the call; after all, you have good skills and believe open, direct communication achieves the best results.	E _____
Take the call, thinking that if the caller gets nasty, you'll get just as tough back.	F _____
	Total = 10

Your coworker, employee, or supervisor yells at you in front of others in a meeting. You:

Say nothing, and try to pretend it didn't happen.	A_____
Take him or her on.	B _____
Make a conciliatory statement such as "I can see your point, but . . ."	C_____
Nod and attempt to act with grace.	D_____
Respond with a "Pardon me?" then say, "Let's move from this stalemate to the real issues."	E _____
Say "Do not talk rudely to me."	F _____
	Total = 10

If you err, it's by:

Pretending a bully's comments don't get to you.	A_____
Handling issues before you're ready or haven't thought things through.	B _____
Trying to make things work for everyone, even if it hurts you.	C_____
Telegraphing that you're scared or nervous.	D_____

Standing your ground.	E ____
Confronting toe-to-toe.	F ____
	Total = 10

When criticized, you:	
Try to pretend it doesn't hurt.	A____
Ask "What do you mean?"	B ____
Try to work things out.	C____
Wonder if it really was your fault, after all.	D____
Ask the critic to clarify his or her thinking.	E ____
Let the critic know not to mess with you.	F ____
	Total = 10

When others disagree with one of your ideas or suggestions, you:	
Listen quietly.	A____
Point out what about your ideas makes sense and what they're not considering.	B ____
See if you can find a way to work things out.	C____
Worry that they'll prevail and consider how you can live with their conclusion.	D____
Listen to their viewpoint, clarify your own, and know that you'll be able to work it out.	E ____
Challenge what's wrong with their viewpoint.	F ____
	Total = 10

When someone you work with is hostile (yells, threatens, uses abusive language), you usually:	
Shut down.	A____
Let the person know she or he shouldn't act that way.	B ____
Try to understand why the person is acting that way.	C____
Worry about what will happen next.	D____
Ask the other person to get to the issues.	E ____
Tell the other person she or he needs to clean it up.	F ____
	Total = 10

When you walk in on a heated argument, you:	
Leave.	A____
Try to see if you can fix things and say what you're thinking.	B ____
Worry about what might happen and try to help everyone work it out.	C____
Hope that things will blow over, particularly if those involved work close to you.	D____
Try to mediate.	E ____
Listen, figure out what's happening, and get into the exchange.	F ____
	Total = 10

When someone takes advantage of you, you:	
Try not to deal with this person again.	A____
Notice what's happening and gently but firmly let the person know you don't intend to let this happen.	B ____

Handle the situation, but don't make waves. C____

Worry that the person will figure out how to take advantage of you while you're not looking. D____

Call the situation as you see it, calmly and without attacking anyone. E____

Tell the person to knock it off. F____

Total = 10

Continued conflict seems to swirl around two employees in the department you manage (please respond to this question even if you aren't a manager). You:

Hope it resolves itself. A____

Meet with each person individually and coach them so they learn the skills to address it themselves. B____

Don't fix the conflict, but try to make each of the employees feel better to alleviate morale problems. C____

Ask each employee about the situation, but back off if either tells you to butt out. D____

Meet with each employee, assess the situation, and bring both employees into your office to mediate and resolve the situation. E____

Bring the two employees into your office and tell them both to knock it off. F____

Total = 10

Conflict:

Makes you sick to your stomach. A____

Is inevitable and something you need to handle. B____

Worries you and is something you hope doesn't occur. C____

Makes you worry about worse consequences, but you know you need to address it. D____

Is simply part of life and although it's problematic, it can also lead to positive change. E ____

Is something you don't mind and can handle, sometimes bluntly. F ____

Total = 10

	A	B	C	D	E	F	
Total points assigned to each letter							= 100

DECODING YOUR INVENTORY

If you have thirty or more points in a style, it's definitely part of your approach to handling conflict. If you have fewer than nine points in a style, it's not an approach you tend to take. You may have thirty or more points in as many as three styles. You may also have relatively equal numbers of points in four or even five styles, or there may be one or two patterns you never choose.

All styles have positive and negative consequences. Some styles have significantly better outcomes; others have significantly worse outcomes. You increase your likelihood of using the right conflict approach when you feel comfortable with multiple styles.

THE STYLES

"A": If you have thirty or more points in "A," you practice avoidance.

Avoidance allows conflicts to fester and escalate. Avoidance can be a legitimate choice temporarily, or for a trivial issue, or if you would derive little or no payoff by heading into the conflict.

Avoidance can take the form of diplomatically sidestepping an issue, postponing dealing with a situation, or withdrawing from a problematic person or situation. Sonja, Suzanne, and Tova, who each gave away their power and became a bully's easy target, all practiced avoidance.

Avoiders most often swallow what they want to say. When confronted, they often say, "Sure," "Okay," and "Whatever you want."

"B": If you have thirty or more points in "B," you choose confrontation.

Confrontation comes from a "let's handle this" perspective. Confronters may use both negative and positive methods; confronting can create both positive and negative consequences.

Mavis confronted Bernard when she prepared a video and threatened to send it to Anderson Cooper, but left Bernard the choice of whether or not he stopped bullying his employees. After HR manager Jess confronted Ray, Ray countered by taking his case to their CEO and accusing Jess of not doing her job.

Confronters often offer the bully a dignified out, as in "Are you sure you want to do this?" Confronters also make comments such as "Let's not go there" and "Let's back up here, and not go toe-to-toe when we can reach an agreement we'll both be happy with."

"C": If you have thirty or more points in "C," you choose accommodation.

Accommodators live with the rules and within the parameters established by others in an effort to preserve harmony and avoid disruption. Accommodators neglect their own concerns to satisfy other people's needs and believe the myth "Mellow your enemies with kindness."

Accommodation proves an excellent choice when the issue matters more to the other person than it does to you, and when a goodwill gesture or a cooling-off period improves one's eventual results. Accommodation can serve as a bandage but is not a permanent fix because although others may feel better, you haven't addressed the underlying conflict. Newly promoted Adam tried to accommodate Geoff by letting Geoff know Adam considered Geoff valuable and wanted things to work out. As Adam learned, if you're an accommodator, you may give up more than you want, and accommodation works only if it leads the other person to positively respond.

Accommodation language includes "I'll go along with this because it matters to you, even though it's not my first or even second choice" and "I can put up with this."

"D": If you have thirty or more points in "D," you move forward fearfully.

Although you act, you worry and telegraph your hesitation to others. Bullies can control you, as you strive to appease them even when you know they're wrong. At the same time, you're headed in the right direction and can grow this style into a more assertive one by honing your skills in each real-life situation.

Maura wound up confronting a bully attorney after she fired an employee who pirated her material. Softhearted Maura told Elliott she wished him well and tried to resolve the conflict by sending him multiple letters "reminding" him the stolen materials weren't his. Although Maura didn't wholeheartedly choose legal action, she learned she could stand firm when she prevailed after a showdown with a scorched-earth bully in front of the judge.

Moving forward with fear language includes, "I know you didn't mean this, but it hurts" and "I wish you wouldn't do this in the future."

"E": If you have thirty or more points in "E," you handle conflict assertively.

You approach conflict in a direct, straightforward manner. You handle issues proactively and not aggressively. Annette handled Andy assertively when she got up and left Andy's office. If you choose "E" consistently, you both watch out for your own interests and respect the rights of others.

Wording that characterizes your "E" style includes "Let's deal with the core issues," "I'm standing my ground," "I know we'll work it out," and "I'm calling the situation as I see it." The "E" style addresses the underlying issues that create conflicts and achieves maximum results in most situations.

"F": If you have thirty or more points in "F," you use a "toe-to-toe," head-on approach.

This style is often selected when managers need to implement unpopular courses of action or you as an individual feel fed up. This power-oriented mode handles conflicts quickly and can work well in emergency situations, yet achieves poor results in most other situations.

Mitch used this strategy in Chapter 7 when he and Mike had a staring contest, ending when Mike jabbed his fingers at Mitch's eyes and Mitch grabbed and twisted Mike's fingers backwards.

People in this category believe that "might makes right" and rarely worry about consequences. Language that characterizes this style includes "Knock it off," "Do not mess with me," and "Tell [him or her] [she or he] needs to clean it up." Occasionally the unresolved issues that remain can unravel the outcome you hope to achieve.

Many bullies have thirty or more points in "F."

LAST BUT NOT LEAST: WHAT TO DO IF YOU WITNESS BULLYING

Are you one of the 28.7 million individuals who, according to the 2014 U.S. Workplace Bullying Survey published by the Workplace

Bullying Institute, witness bullying in the workplace on an ongoing basis?[1]

Have you spoken up or intervened? Or do you believe it's not your place to speak up?

It is. If you don't, who will?

Silent witnesses send bullies and those they bully a message. Your silence and inaction colludes with bullies and tells them you fear them or sanction their actions. Your silence sends a worse message to those they bully. It says you don't care how they're treated, and that you agree they deserve to be bullied.

When you speak up or intervene, you say "I don't tolerate bullying." You tell the victim you care. Your action also tells the bully you don't intend to become the next target, a wise preventative action given that the 2014 VitalSmarts survey documents that 80 percent of bullies affect five or more individuals.[2]

If you fear that speaking up may lead the bully to turn on you, overcome your fear and speak up now. It may be just a matter of time before the bully takes you on even if you remain silent. Bullies attack the easiest prey first. Speaking up deflects rather than attracts a bully's interest. If you don't want to speak directly to the bully, seek out a senior manager or a member of your organization's human resources staff.

Your Turn: Where Are You Now?

1. How accurately did your scores on the Curry Conflict Inventory reflect how you handle conflict?
2. What did you learn from the results?
3. Were there any surprises?
4. Have you been a conflict avoider in the past? Has reading *Beating the Workplace Bully* made you less so?
5. What changes do you plan to make in how you handle con-

flict in the future? What's your plan? If you haven't created a conflict-handling goal and game plan yet, use the steps in Chapter 22 to develop one that you'll implement.

6. Have you witnessed bullying?
7. Are you a silent witness? If so, what message do you send? How does your lack of action sanction bullying?
8. What message do you want to send the bully and the individual currently targeted?
9. Is now the time to intervene? If not now, what are you waiting for?
10. Does it take courage for you to speak up? How can you summon that courage?
11. If you plan to report the bullying to someone other than the bully, to whom will you speak? Make an appointment with that individual today.

IT'S TIME TO CELEBRATE!

What's changed since you picked up this book? Have you opened your mind to new insights and possibilities? Has doing the exercises restored your self-worth? Have you discovered more of who you are? The future is bright. Not without risk, but with promise.

It's your turn.

NOTES

1. Gary Namie, 2014 WBI U.S. Workplace Bullying Survey, February 2014, http://www.workplacebullying.org/wbiresearch/wbi-2014-us-survey.
2. Naomi Shavin, "What Workplace Bullying Looks Like in 2014—and How to Intervene," workplace bullying study by David Maxfield and Joseph Grenny, *Forbes*, June 25, 2014, http://www.forbes.com/sites/naomishavin/2014/06/25/what-work-place-bullying-looks-like-in-2014-and-how-to-intervene.

INDEX

ABOUT THE AUTHOR

Lynne Curry founded and runs Alaska's largest management and HR consulting firm, with 3,500 clients in fourteen states, as well as Japan, Korea, England, and China. Armed with a doctorate in social psychology and having earned a Senior Professional in Human Resources certificate, she provides executive and life coaching; manager, employee, and board training; HR on-call services; and mediation, team-building, strategic planning, investigation, and other management consulting services to individuals and organizations. Her clients have included the U.S. Army, ConocoPhillips, the State of Alaska, British Petroleum, Veterans Affairs, and Wells Fargo.

Lynne has authored three earlier books, *Solutions*, *Won by One*, and *Managing Equally and Legally*. Her weekly "Dear Abby of the workplace" column has run since 1983 and hundreds of media outlets from Yahoo! News to CBS MoneyWatch have published her writing.

Lynne has three children, Ben, Jenny, and (angel) Joey, and one granddaughter and divides her time between her home in Anchorage and her cabin in Moose Pass.

Connect with Curry:
Her blog: www.workplacecoachblog.com
Her company: www.thegrowthcompany.com
Twitter: @lynnecurry10